The Secret of *Emotions*

The Secret of Emotions

The Spiritual Roots of Our Hidden Motivations

Justice Saint Rain

Book 1 of the
Love, Lust and the Longing for God trilogy,
which includes:
Four Tools of Emotional Healing
&
Longing for Love

SPECIAL ♥ IDEAS

Special Ideas
511 Diamond Rd Heltonville IN 47436
1-800-326-1197

The Secret of Emotions

By Justice Saint Rain

This book may be purchased individually at
Amazon.com or purchased both individually and in
bulk at www.secretofemotions.com or
www.interfaithresources.com

Other books by Justice Saint Rain

Why Me? A Spiritual Guide to Growing Through Tests
The Secret of Happiness
A Spiritual Guide to Great Sex
Falling Into Grace
My Bahá'í Faith
The Hard Way – Lessons Learned
from the Economic Collapse

Printed in the USA

ISBN 978-1888547-51-1

To all of the people who are
longing to call a truce
in the battle
between
the head
and the heart.

Book 1

Introduction:

If following your heart has repeatedly gotten you into trouble, but to follow your head feels like a kind of soul-death, then this book will open up a whole new world of possibilities for you. It will teach your head how to understand the language of your heart, and teach your heart how to speak the language of God.

You see, I believe that our emotional sensations tell us about the virtues we are experiencing, and that these virtues are reflections of the qualities of God in the world. Making the connection between emotions and virtues gives us a whole new vocabulary for understanding our feelings.

Since most people make their life-choices based on their feelings rather than reason, understanding the meaning of our emotions is the *second*-most important lesson we can learn in this life.

The *most* important lesson is that *virtues are our path to the Transcendent*. Whether you call it God, Higher Power, Creative Spirit, or just your better self, we are all born with a longing to become more than we are right now – to demonstrate that we are, indeed, created in the image of the Divine.

So this book has the humble goal of helping you accurately identify your feelings so that you can develop the virtues that will help you become the best person possible. Along the way, you will heal old wounds, overcome shame, learn the true meaning of love, let go of compulsive behaviors, break unhealthy relationship patterns and develop new, healthy habits that will make future growth even easier.

If all of this seems too much to promise, I offer you this observation: simple awareness is often curative. Understanding the source and meaning of your emotions can literally change everything *in a heartbeat*.

Acknowledgements

Many thanks to the people who read early copies of this work and gave invaluable feedback: Phyllis Edgerly Ring, editor, and the author of *Life at First Sight – Finding the Divine in the Details*; Phyllis K. Peterson, author of *Remaining Faithful*; Kim Bowden-Kerby, whose advice was worth much more than I paid for it; and Jay Cardwell who found more in it than I put in.

Thanks, also, to all of the readers of my earlier works whose support and encouragement made the publication of this book possible.

This is **book one** in the *Longing for God* trilogy that also includes *Four Tools of Emotional Healing* and *Longing for Love*. Watch for the other two parts available soon, or get all three in the complete book, *Love, Lust and the Longing for God* that includes additional material and resources.

Book 1
The Secret of *Emotions*

We are all born with an innate longing for God – not a god with a long white beard who shakes his finger at us, but the Divine Creative Spirit that blessed the universe with breathtaking wonder and touched our hearts with limitless grace.

This God filled His creation with His most noble attributes—and then placed the potential for each of these qualities within the human heart. Our longing for God is not an intellectual longing. It is a *spiritual* longing. We approach God, not through theological study, but by being attracted to the attributes of God that are both reflected in creation and placed within our hearts. It is these attributes, then, such as love, beauty, honesty, forgiveness, patience, creativity and compassion that are the source of our longing for God.

Of all of the attributes that we long for, the one that pulls at our hearts most strongly is love. It is the one we sing songs about; the one we organize our lives around; the one that we are absolutely sure will solve all of our problems.

One would think, then, that over the course of thousands of years we would all have come to a clear understanding of what love is, how it feels in our hearts, and how true *spiritual* love differs from its more material counterparts of lust and passion. Yet we have not.

Almost no one has.

Our inability to understand and accurately identify love causes many of us to do things in the name of love that are anything but loving; things that take us farther from our goals instead of nearer to them; things that make us feel ashamed instead of noble; things that convince us that we are failures instead of the radiant children of God that we are.

If we are ever going to satisfy our longing for love, and live the lives we were meant to live, then we will need to find a way to accurately identify spiritual love when we experience it so that we can create more of it in our lives.

This is the golden ring.
This is what we all want.

But it is bigger than that.
In order to learn how to recognize *one* of God's attributes, we must develop the understanding and skills needed to recognize *all of them*. God is not a grab-bag of isolated gifts, like faith, hope and love that you get to pick and choose. God is One. If you want to tap into God's love, you have to be prepared to accept *all* of God's bounties, and if you want to be able to recognize and create one virtue, you will need to develop the skills to recognize and create them all – not all at once, but as a lifelong process.

That process, I believe, begins by getting our hearts, our minds and our bodies all speaking the same language so that what we want, what we feel and what we know all fit together accurately and are in harmony with one another.

When our spiritual, physical and intellectual sides understand and respect each other, then we become whole. We are no longer divided against ourselves. We become the pilots of our own lives rather than being buffeted by needs, wants and sensations that confuse us, sabotage our best intentions and lead us astray.

You see, none of us wants a series of dysfunctional relationships. We don't want to destroy our marriages, sit alone in dark rooms watching videos, fantasize about people who will never love us, or do any of the other things that cause us shame. And yet if that is what we find in our lives, *that must be what we are pursuing.* Why is it, then, that we spend time and energy trying to acquire something that isn't what we really want?

What is it that we are looking for when we walk into that bar, pick up that phone, log onto that website, smile at that stranger or knock on that door?

The answer is…

The answer ALWAYS is…

God.

We are looking for God manifested in the world of creation.

We are looking for love, kindness, meaning, security, joy, hope, nobility, connection, and a myriad other virtues that God deposited within the human heart when He made it His home.

But if that is what we are looking for…

Why can't we find it?

The answer, if you think about it, is pretty obvious: Because we don't know what these qualities look like, or, more accurately, we don't know what these qualities FEEL like when we encounter them. How could we know how to accurately identify the signs of God's virtues, when everyone out there is as confused as we are? We mistake kindness for weakness, hope for naïveté, nobility for stuffiness, and love… well love is the most misidentified virtue of all. We have been given wildly inaccurate and misleading information about this most important of virtues by everyone – from our families, schools, and religious communities, to almost every single movie and pop song ever made. The feelings we mistake for love range from need and lust to pity, fear and shame.

I can say this because at different times in my life, I've mistaken each of these sensations for love, and I don't think I'm alone. If you have your doubts, let me describe a few experiences and see if they sound familiar. Then I'll describe what I have come to believe love really is and how it really feels. But first, the mistakes:

My Rosetta Stone

This is the story of how I became painfully aware that I had absolutely no idea of what my emotional sensations were trying to tell me.

During my last year of college, I was dating someone pretty seriously. She was an absolutely wonderful woman – one with whom I might have been happy my entire life. We had talked about marriage, but this was several years before her graduation so we hadn't become "officially" engaged or set a date.

One weekend, I went home to visit friends. While there, my best friend, who was married, told me about a wonderful single woman who had recently joined the community. He encouraged me to check her out before making any final commitments to my girlfriend.

I went to visit her, and had one of the strangest experiences of my entire life. Sitting in her room, my entire body began to tingle. I felt like I had electricity running through my veins. I remember that when she left the room for a minute, I paced back and forth, shaking my arms and fingers, trying to fling the excess energy out of my body. I was sure that if I touched her, sparks would fly between us.

Surely, this was a sign from God.

My heart was beating, my body tingled from head to toe; this must be what love was supposed to feel like.

Even though I knew almost nothing about this woman, I went back to my girlfriend and confessed that I would not be able to commit to getting married to her until I had explored this new relationship. She looked me in the eye and said, "Get out."

So I moved back home to see if I could turn sparks and tingles into a permanent relationship. As you might guess, over the next few months the sparks and tingles began to fade, and when I was offered a job in a different city, our relationship died a natural death.

I was befuddled. What had it all been about?

Fast forward almost exactly ten years. I am divorced, broke, depressed, alone and horny. I find myself in the middle of the night, standing in the parking lot of an adult video store. As I contemplate whether or not to go in, my body starts to tingle. I feel like I have electricity running through my veins. I start shaking my arms and fingers, trying to fling some of that excess energy out of my body.

I stop.

I remember this feeling.

But now it sure doesn't feel like love.

What was it all about?

I now had two data points for one sensation. What did they have in common? It wasn't love. It wasn't sex (I hadn't been contemplating sex with the woman I had just met). So what were my heart and body trying to tell my short-circuited brain?

Finally, after much time, prayer, journaling and therapy, I figured it out.

This is what intense shame feels like.

I was ashamed of myself for being untrue to my girlfriend.

I was ashamed of myself for thinking of buying pornography.

My body had been trying to tell me to turn around and run, and what I heard was, "This is really, really important. Stay and explore it."

If I could so completely misidentify a message of shame as a message of love, what *other* sensations had I misidentified over the years?

I began to listen, and watch, and correlate sensations with the experiences that went with them.

I discovered that when I got weak in the knees, it didn't mean I was in love. It meant that I was afraid that I would be blamed for breaking someone's heart.

I discovered that when my heart was moved by a woman's tears, it wasn't love, but a desire to rescue someone.

Over time, I began to identify sensations that were so subtle that I couldn't put a name to them, I could only identify them by the patterns they followed.

A certain tug on my heart let me know that women had been sexually abused.

A similar tug said that they were afraid of men.

Another told me that they were recently divorced with small children at home.

An uneasiness that at one time might have felt exciting now tells me that someone is not being completely honest.

At one point, all of these little emotional cues – whispers of the heart – would have been interpreted as, "God wants me to explore a relationship with this person." Now these messages simply say, "This person reflects some aspect of my relationship to my original God-figure. Resolve that relationship, don't enter into this one."

❀

Recalibrating Our Inner Compass

Each of us is born with many wonderful capacities, but very little information, and even less understanding of how to make sense of that information. We have the capacity to see, for example, but it takes months for us to recognize faces, and years before we can make the distinction between pink and purple. We could say that parents and children work together to calibrate the child's visual perception so that the child not only sees, but understands what it sees and can distinguish between similar sensory cues.

We are also born with an inner compass. Instead of visual sensory input, we use spiritual emotional input to point us towards the many attributes of God in our environment. We learn to recognize love, kindness, joy, respect, compassion, security, patience, and a host of other qualities through our innate emotional attraction to their presence.

Just as our physical senses need to be trained, so do our spiritual senses. They need input, and that input needs to be calibrated against some kind of standard – a base against which all input is measured. For a baby, its inner compass is calibrated to point towards the god-figure in its life – its parents, particularly its mother. Just as we are born with the ability to see, but are taught to give names and meanings to the things we see, we are born with the ability to feel, but we are taught, mostly by our parents, how to give names and meanings to our feelings.

If your parent didn't know the difference between pink and any other random light color, you would have gone to kindergarten calling every pastel color "pink." Likewise, if your parent didn't know the difference between love and other strong spiritual sensations, then you would learn to look for love every time your heart or your body tried to send you a message, regardless of what that message was. This is how many of us come to interpret *any* intense sensation as a signal that we are falling in love.

It is also possible that your parents had a very clear image of what love is all about, but it just wasn't accurate. In this case, you would consciously or unconsciously, absorb your parent's expectations about love, and associate love with any number of unhealthy sensations.

If, for example, your parent said, "I love you" as they punished you, or ignored you, or laid guilt on you, or shamed you, or clung to you, or abused you, then *your* search for God will probably lead you towards people and activities that generate the sensations associated with these feelings. And when you find them, you will probably *think* that you are head-over-heels in love.

As children, we have an innate need to believe that our care-givers love us, and we will go to great lengths to reinterpret anything and everything they do as an expression of love. So *however* you were treated as a child, *that* is your core-level definition of love, no matter how many layers of intellectual calibrating you have done since then. It is important to change your conscious understanding of what love is. It is even more important to re-educate your subconscious emotional responses so that your heart doesn't drag you, kicking and screaming, where your head knows not to go.

Of course, this realization is not really anything new. Most people are aware that they learned about relationships from their parents. What is helpful about this framing of the idea is that it focuses not just on an abstract intellectual lesson learned, but on the *sensations* that we subconsciously learned to associate with God, love, and the goal of our desire. It then relates these sensations to the virtues that are the true goal of our search.

Understanding the relationship between virtues and emotions gives us a new and valuable tool in accurately identifying the meaning behind our emotional sensations. This tool can be used by both the mind *and* the heart and can help establish harmony between them.

So if we ask our original question again – "Why can't we find what we are looking for?" the answer is that we DO find what we are looking for, but what we are looking for is not what we really want. What we are looking for is things that remind us of the god of our childhood, but this god was not an accurate guide to the virtues and sensations that we really want.

If we want to start finding GOD, with a capital G, as manifested in holy virtues like love, kindness, patience, and serenity, then we will have to recalibrate our inner compass.

We will have to correlate the sensations we experience with a more accurate and objective assessment of the virtues we are experiencing. We will have to learn to distinguish between fool's gold and true gold, between lust, pity, need or fear – and love.

Then, finally, we will have to fall in love with the *real* virtues that are reflections of God and that reside in our own hearts. When we learn to love what is real and true, our obsessions with imitation love and the sensations surrounding it will fade.

❁

The Importance of Emotions

"God conceals himself from the mind of man, but reveals himself to his heart."   — *African Proverb*

Most of us understand on a gut-level that emotions are important. They need to be listened to. But we don't understand *why*, and so we alternate between ignoring our emotions, and following them blindly.

In a piece called "The New Humanism," New York Times columnist David Brooks described the importance of combining reason and emotion and noted that: "…our emotions assign value to things and are the basis of reason."

That is a great phrase: *emotions assign value to things*, but there is no explanation as to how or why. When we figure out how and why emotions are important and how they assign value, then we will be in a better position to figure out *what* they are telling us, and *when* to listen to them.

This is what I believe: our emotions are spiritual sensations that tell us about the presence or absence of virtues in our lives, and virtues are the attributes of God expressed in the world of creation. Since our purpose in life is to develop these virtues within ourselves, it is only natural that we have been given the tools to recognize them when they are present.

Not only is it *natural* that we would be given this amazing ability to perceive our spiritual environment, but it is absolutely necessary. How else could we be expected to love the attributes of God in the world, if we were not given the ability to perceive them? If all we had to rely on was our intellectual capacity, then love, kindness, beauty, harmony, and joy would be dry intellectual or philosophical exercises – outside the experience of the vast majority of humanity.

We all know this is not how life works. The ability to recognize kindness, patience and fairness is not bestowed upon those with superior intellects. It is given to those with pure hearts.

It is the heart, then, that has been created with the capacity to recognize these divine qualities. And what tool does the heart have to communicate its recognition of a spiritual quality other than the spiritual emotions?

It is this innate awareness that our emotions are our means of recognizing and celebrating the attributes of God in the world that makes us choose to follow the promptings of our hearts – even when we don't understand them.

As we come to understand a little of what the heart is trying to communicate, we can begin to create an emotional glossary of terms that correlates the sensations that we feel with the virtues that we observe. Eventually, this glossary will be rich enough and complete enough to allow real communication between our heads and our hearts.

❀

Physical Emotions and Spiritual Emotions

When the heart becomes whole, it will know the flavors of falsehood and truth.   — *Rumi*

One of the things that complicates our ability to identify our emotions accurately is the fact that our minds, hearts and bodies influence each other, but not always in a helpful way. We have physical emotions, which respond to physical threats and stimuli, and spiritual emotions that respond to our spiritual environment, and a mind that tries to figure out what these similar yet different sources of sensations are trying to say.

I like to compare the relationship between physical emotions and spiritual emotions to the relationship between taste and smell. When you combine the sensation of taste on your tongue with the sensation of smell through your nose, you experience a flavor. Likewise, when you combine your physical response to a situation with your spiritual response to a situation, you experience the "emotional flavor" of the situation. The two work together to give you a more complete and satisfying understanding of what is going on.

To appreciate this analogy, it helps to understand how taste and smell work together. This is how Wikipedia explains it:

Of the three chemical senses, smell is the main determinant of a food item's flavor. While the taste of food is limited to sweet, sour, bitter, salty, and savory – the basic tastes – the smells of a food are potentially limitless. [Our perception of] a food's flavor, therefore, can be easily altered by changing its smell while keeping its taste similar.

Comparing physical emotions to taste and spiritual emotions to smell offers several insights. First, it illustrates the fact that our bodies have a limited range of responses to any given situation, but our spirits have an almost unlimited capacity to distinguish between different virtues that may be present.

Second, when we think of a flavor, we prioritize the experience of its taste on our tongue, even though for most flavors, it is the smell that imparts the most pleasure and information. Likewise, when we think of emotions, we often focus on our physical reaction to a situation. This is why researchers often limit their study of emotions to the handful that can be measured biochemically. In doing this, they ignore the fact that it is our spiritual response that distinguishes between the similar sensations of excitement and fear, between patience and boredom, between feeling hungry and feeling empty.

When we over-emphasize the importance of our physical emotional responses, we minimize the role that our mind and heart play in generating emotions. What we *think* makes a big difference in what we *feel*.

If you were handed a piece of red candy and told it was strawberry – and if it smelled like strawberry, you would have a very difficult time determining whether the actual taste was grape, cherry, or even chocolate! What we see, smell and hear can change what we taste.

Likewise, if you are about to go on stage to give a talk and you tell yourself, "I'm so scared. I'm so scared!" you can easily work yourself into a full-blown panic attack. On the other hand, if you tell yourself, "This is so exciting. This is so exciting!" you can walk out on stage with confidence and enthusiasm. So one experience can generate two very different feelings depending on what we tell ourselves.

This is because the physical symptoms of fear and excitement are almost exactly the same. There is not enough information in the physical sensation to tell us what is really going on. All we know is that we need to wake up and pay attention.

It is what we *tell ourselves* about the sensation that points it in one direction or another. Once you define the sensation for yourself, your spirit and your body will create a reinforcing feedback loop.

I've already talked about how easy it is to convince ourselves that we are in love when we are really experiencing shame. The other strong physical sensation that we often tell ourselves is love is really *fear*. Fear tells our body to wake up. What we tell ourselves after that determines whether our bodies produce more adrenaline or more pheromones. If we tell ourselves we are attracted to someone, then our bodies will start generating arousal rather than a fight or flight response. Once that happens, it is easy to convince ourselves that what we felt from the very beginning was attraction. I will talk about this more after I describe what I believe true love really is.

※

Understanding Love

Love is metaphysical gravity.   — *R. Buckminster Fuller*

The power which moves, controls and attracts the hearts of men is the love of God.   — *'Abdu'l-Bahá*

If we want to recognize true love instead of being fooled by shame, fear, pity, need, and all of the other imitations we have been taught to accept, then we probably ought to have an accurate working definition of the term.

I will start by explaining my understanding of what real love is, and then contrast that with the experience of *romantic* love, or being *in* love.*

Real Love

Pieces of iron are innately attracted to a magnet. Flowers in a garden naturally turn towards the light of the sun. When we walk through that garden, we are instinctively drawn to bend down and smell the sweetness of a rose.

The heart is naturally attracted to the signs of God in the world.

This attraction – this innate tendency to turn towards beauty, kindness, enthusiasm and generosity – is the essence of love.

When we look around the world, the best reflections of these qualities can be found in the human soul.

In book 3 of this series there is a chapter, Sensations We Mistake for Love, in which I describe other facets of love, along with the many emotional sensations that masquerade as love.

Human love, then, is simply the recognition of, admiration for and attraction to the attributes of God in another person.

This attraction is felt in the heart. It is warm and pleasant, and grows with increased interaction. It is rarely overwhelming, and can be felt for people of any age, race or sex.

If we have learned to love such attributes as kindness, patience, responsibility, and joyfulness, then we will recognize, appreciate and be attracted to these qualities when we see them expressed in a human being — no matter who the person may be.

How much we love a person is determined by our ability to recognize virtues when we experience them, the strength of our attraction to those virtues, and the number and quality of virtues that the person expresses.

Take a look at that definition again. It is simple and universal, but it may contradict your long-held beliefs about love. You may, for example, want to separate love into several sub categories like romantic love, brotherly love and parental love. Or you may want to define love by the *things we do* as a result of feeling love – things like psychologist Erich Fromm's *care, responsibility, respect* and *knowledge* from his book *The Art of Loving*, or Scott Peck's *the will to extend oneself for the purpose of nurturing one's own or another's spiritual growth.* You might associate love with many of the intense feelings that masquerade as love, such as passion, attachment or need.

Rather than either wrestling with this definition now, or accepting it outright, I invite you to set your current understanding aside for a while and see where this approach takes you. You can always pick it back up later.

This definition of love focuses on a person's qualities rather than his or her personality, and on our attraction to those qualities rather than the actions that are the result of that attraction. What does it mean to be attracted to a *quality* rather than a person? Let's take as examples two of the qualities I've been mentioning: kindness and responsibility.

Experiencing someone's kindness generates a sensation. It feels good just to watch a person showing kindness, even if it is towards someone else. If we are attracted to kindness – if we see it as a sign of strength instead of weakness – then our *attraction* will *also* generate a sensation. It feels like the invisible pull of a magnet. When the sensation of attraction combines with the sensation of kindness, they reinforce one another to a point that it is impossible to ignore or dismiss. The strength of the combined sensation can spill over into a general positive regard for the person expressing this attractive virtue.

The virtue of responsibility also generates sensations. Watching a person make wise and thoughtful decisions in the face of temptations to do otherwise can be very uplifting, and yet not as many people are aware of these sensations because they have not been taught to recognize and be attracted to them. Without the attraction, the sensations go unnoticed and are not reinforced. They therefore do not spill over into a general appreciation for the person demonstrating responsibility. If we don't love the qualities a person demonstrates, it is difficult to feel that we love them, no matter how wonderful they may be.

It is our ability to be attracted to positive qualities, then, that expands our ability to love the people around us. This means that the more virtues we learn to recognize and be attracted to, the more people we will love, and the more rewarding our interaction with them will be.

If we learn to be attracted to even a *hint* of a virtue, or even just the *potential* for a virtue, then we can find a way to love almost anyone. The ability to love *potential* is what makes a parent's love for their children come so naturally.

Though virtues are universal, each individual has developed a unique collection of virtues and expresses them in their own way. I like to think of virtues as stars, and individuals have their own constellations of qualities that create the patterns of their lives. We don't just love the individual points of light; we take pleasure in discovering the patterns that they form as they blaze their arc across the heavens.

The Limitations of Love as a Sensation

It is a good thing that love feels good. When we discover the signs of God in another person – courage, wisdom, kindness, responsibility – then it is helpful that our hearts respond with a positive sensation that attracts us to this person and those qualities. The sensation is a message that says, "Look this way! Notice this person! Learn from these qualities!" The sensation makes us enjoy spending time with this person and lets us know that we have found someone worth investing time and attention in.

But a message is just a message. Once the message has been delivered, there is no need for it to stand around whispering in your ear. The sensations of love need not last forever.

Think of love as a fragrance. When you step into a person's life, you smell the fragrance and it pleases you. But in time, your ability to smell that particular fragrance fades. It is not that the fragrance has gone away, but your need to smell it, and therefore your *ability* to smell it has disappeared.

Now, if a completely *different* fragrance enters the room, then *that* is what you will notice. Perhaps the person you love smells like kindness, responsibility and patience, but now someone who smells like creativity and courage steps into your life. If you believe that the most important thing about love is its ability to generate sensations, then you will believe that you no longer love the first person and now only love the second.

The truth is, you may love them both. The question is, which have you made a commitment to? When you understand how love, sensations and virtues relate to one another, then you know that commitment trumps sensation almost every time.

Knowing that sensations fade over time, we can do two things: 1) minimize the importance we give to sensations, and 2) never lose interest in our partners. If we keep growing and keep exploring one another's character, then we will continue to discover new virtues, new potentials, new capacities that will awaken new sensations of appreciation and attraction.

Romantic Love

There are many sensations that we mistake for love, but there are only a few that create that intense, overwhelming feeling that we associate with *romantic* love. One is shame, which I've already mentioned and will discuss in detail later. Another is *fear*.

The sensations that are usually associated with feeling "in love" – nervousness, butterflies in the stomach, weak knees, obsessive thinking, or light headedness – have little or nothing to do with love. If you felt these sensations while sitting next to an 800 pound gorilla rather than an attractive person, then you would recognize them for the symptoms of *terror* that they really are.

Why, you ask, would you feel fear when in the presence of an attractive person, and how could you possibly mistake fear for love?

I'll start with the second question. We don't recognize fear because it makes no logical sense. It is not what we expect, so we can't recognize it. What we *expect* is what every movie, song, story and friend has told us about this feeling: a fluttering heart is a sign of true love. In the face of such overwhelming evidence, your mind overrides your intuition and you call the feeling love.

Many years ago, for example, I found myself getting weak in the knees while kissing a new girlfriend, so I called an old friend and asked what she thought it might mean. She said she still got weak in the knees sometimes when kissing her husband of 15 years. I took this as a good sign and entered the relationship with high hopes and great enthusiasm. Two months later, my new relationship ended because of serious trust issues. How could this be? My knees had told me I could have a romantic relationship like my friend's. As it turned out, I did. "Weak knees" did not save my friend's marriage either. It was their *belief* in the significance of weak knees that had kept them together, but they had been secretly unhappy for years.

The answer to the question of how we can mistake fear for love, then, is quite simple. Even our best friends will tell us that fear is really love – because almost everyone believes it.

America's Classic Romance

Love is a light that never dwelleth in a heart possessed by fear.
— *Bahá'u'lláh*

Perhaps you have heard of this classic romance – one that has sold millions of books and sent mothers and daughters to theaters together to swoon over its depiction of true love. It is about Bella, a pretty, but klutzy and socially awkward girl who is literally swept off her feet by the handsome, charming, very strong and *very* mysterious Edward. The minor problem in their affair is that he, unfortunately, is a vampire.

Given this situation, what would be the appropriate sensation for Bella to feel? Fear, of course. But Edward also manages to save her life using his superhuman strength, which makes him her savior. Thus he is both the source of her fear and the source of her protection from fear at the same time. The more they are together, the more she needs his protection. We can certainly understand the intensity of her feelings in his presence, but who in their right mind would call this love? Well, actually, every Disney movie for the last 50 years has confused love with being rescued, and several, such as The Beauty and the Beast, include the element of danger to intensify the sensation.

Edward, on the other hand, gets to feel a host of complementary intense feelings around Bella. First, there is the obvious sense of power he gets from protecting her (she is such a klutz that she is *always* needing protection). But this savior role is countered by the guilt he feels for putting her in danger in the first place, and his shame over being a vampire. What seals the deal, however, is the fact that, though vampires can read human's minds, he is unable to read hers. This makes her the most mysterious human he's ever met.

How many other times have we seen men fall for the mysterious "other" or the vulnerable person they want to protect? These paths to love are depicted over and over in movies and literature. Yes, it feels good to take care of people, and it is convenient that our imaginations can fill in the spaces in the mysterious unknown with whatever we hope might be there. But what do these things have to do with love?

When we don't understand what our feelings are trying to tell us, all we have to go on is their intensity. We then equate intensity with significance, and cling to the intensity in the hope of making our relationships and our lives seem more significant.

Bella and Edward's relationship was written to elicit the maximum intensity of feelings, but nowhere in their inter-actions were there any indications that those feelings had anything to do with an attraction to each other's spiritual virtues. And yet, for millions of readers, this story was not about fear, vulnerability, salvation, guilt and mystery, it was about *love*.

Back to you…

But you aren't in love with a vampire, so why would *you* feel fear in the presence of an attractive person in the first place? What is it about the people you are attracted to that you fear, and why would your heart recognize someone as dangerous before your mind did? If emotions tell us about virtues, where are the virtues?

Emotions tell us about our spiritual environment, which includes the presence and the *absence* of virtues. Our eyes see light, but they can also experience darkness. Our skin feels warmth, but it must also be able to respond to cold. Our stomachs can tell us when they are full, but are most insistent when they are empty. Our hearts are filled by the presence of love and kindness and faithfulness, but when they are empty, they are saddened by the lack of these things and feel the loss.

Just as our stomachs growl when empty without us tell-ing them to, and our eyes can see colors whether we know the name for them or not, our hearts often respond to our spiri-tual surroundings without our making a conscious choice or using intellectual cues. When we feel that we "know" some-thing without knowing why or how we know it, we often call it intuition, but that doesn't mean it is magic. We are simply using a kind of spiritual perception that we didn't know we had.

When you meet a person, some part of you is capable of recognizing the presence or absence of key spiritual qualities in them almost instantly. When it recognizes wonderful, loving, nurturing qualities, then you naturally respond with the warm, pleasant, heart-centered feelings described in the first section on love.

When it recognizes qualities that have caused you pain in the past – ones expressed by parents, siblings, teachers or previous relationships – then it experiences fear. This is not to say that these people are *evil*, only that they are *familiar* in a way that feels unsafe. Perhaps they are simply needy, or shaming, or are afraid of commitment. Because of the close relationship between the heart and body, this fear interacts with the body to release adrenaline and other chemicals. These chemicals cause the heart to pound and the stomach to tighten. Physical senses become more focused and intense, *but higher reasoning functions become blurred*.

If this fight-or-flight response is redefined as love, then you are left in a very vulnerable position. Your mind is telling your heart to start looking for things to love, so your heart tells your body to gear up, not for running, but for flirting. Consequently, all of that adrenaline is redirected towards arousal. You are now more susceptible to sexual stimulation (sensual and hormonal), and are less able to reason your way out of obviously compromising situations. This is how most unhealthy relationships begin.

Why do we stay?

Once you are physically separated from this person, these sensations will naturally fade, so why doesn't your better judgment kick in and point you towards someone less scary? There are two reasons. First, as I've said, these are the people whom your mind tells you are exciting, stimulating and sexy. Everyone is looking for their Bella or Edward.

But there is a deeper reason.

The purpose of life is to learn and grow. We learn when we face challenges and overcome them. Challenges that we faced when we were very young sometimes overcame *us*. We did not have the mental, physical or spiritual resources we needed in order to successfully overcome certain recurring trauma. If, as adults, we do not *consciously* seek out and work through these issues, then we will *subconsciously* recognize and be attracted to them when we least expect it. If we are lucky, we will recognize these people as learning experiences instead of marrying them.

It is a truism that when the thrill of romance (adrenaline) wears off, most people discover that they have married one of their parents. This is because a disapproving parent is what our souls fear most, and therefore respond to most intensely. We call these relationships *dealing with unfinished business.*

Recently, an acquaintance came up to me at a conference, wanting to tell me why she absolutely *had* to marry her new husband. You see, it seems that the first time she hugged him, the heavens opened up and the angels sang – for both of them. So even though she didn't want to get married, and it made no sense, she could not go against the will of God and refuse his offer.

Since I have great respect for this person, I was willing to consider the possibility that in this one instance, this was a sign of true love.

Then she ended with the statement: "hugging him felt just like hugging my father."

Her father… who I knew to be a wonderful man, was also a manic depressive who had divorced her mother when she was young. He left a hole in her life that had not yet been filled.

Who am I to stand in the way of unfinished business?

Why We Marry Our Mothers

We don't always enter into unhealthy relationships because we have misidentified a sensation as love.

Sometimes we are drawn into unhealthy relationships because we are subconsciously attempting to *reenact* situations,
failures, traumas and problems that caused us stress in the past.

Now this might sound like some really heavy psychologi-
cal mumbo-jumbo, but it is really pretty basic and easy to
demonstrate.

Have you ever been in a situation where someone insulted
you or embarrassed you, and you couldn't think of the right
thing to say or do to save face right at that moment? Physically, your heart probably started beating faster, your body
released adrenaline, and you felt physically agitated. Soon af-
terwards, you started mentally reliving the experience, trying
to think of the right thing to say, or imagining the right physical response to prevent or rescue the situation.

How *soon* after the experience did you start thinking of
alternative scenarios? How *long* after the situation were you
still running through alternative responses? Was it minutes?
Hours? Days? Perhaps months or years?

Chances are that the more adrenaline your body released
during the stressful situation, the more times you relived the
scene in your mind. Also, the more helpless you felt in the
face of the humiliation, the more important the mental reliving is, and the wilder the fantasized victory over the other
person will be.

This reliving process is completely natural. It applies to
sports, video games, business transactions, failed romances,
marital battles, and any other situation in which the mental,
"If only I had…" kicks in after the fact.

This is how we learn. We remember difficult situations or
mistakes that we have made, try to imagine how we might
respond differently, and mentally rehearse this response in
preparation for our next encounter. When a similar situation
does arise, our bodies will respond with the same fight-or-
flight excitement, but our minds will be better prepared to
handle the challenge effectively.

In most day-to-day activities, this process serves us well. We visualize ourselves catching the football we dropped, or double-checking our work before submitting an assignment, or making some clever comment in a social situation. Reliving, imagining and rehearsing works when we possess the capacity to make things work out better the next time.

But what if we don't?

When we were humiliated, abused, insulted, or placed in difficult situations as *children*, there was little we could do to make things better the next time. The details of the situation may have changed from day to day, but the core dynamic — powerful adult interacting with powerless child — remained the same for years at a time. When we were hurt, we didn't feel safe enough to challenge the situation, but that didn't mean we weren't reliving it over and over. Each time we would try to imagine what it would take to make things better. Did we need to become big, strong and powerful like Superman to protect ourselves, or beautiful and perfect like a princess so no one would want to hurt us? The possibilities were as endless as our imaginations.

Because, as children, we never felt safe enough or powerful enough to challenge the people who hurt us directly, the fantasy reenactment that we rehearsed never got acted out. Consequently, it will *stay* a fantasy until we grow up and find a safe substitute on which to try out our response.

That safe substitute can be anyone who reminds us of the original stressful situation, but who does not have as much power to hurt us as the original offender.

The right person might not appear in our lives until much of the original pain has been consciously forgotten. But *consciously* forgotten is not the same as gone.

Most events in our lives happen only once. The painful ones that we think we could have changed are recreated in our minds dozens, hundreds, perhaps thousands of times. Many become so painful that we tuck them below the surface of our memory until we meet a person that reminds us of our past.

The problem is that we don't consciously know that this person reminds us of anything. The remembering that takes place is not an intellectual remembering. It is an emotional recognition of the familiar. When our hearts recognize a familiar pattern of behavior, they generate the appropriate emotional sensations, which are then communicated to the body.

Those sensations, so often mistaken for love, are really trying to tell us that *something important is going on here.*

This is not mysterious. This is not magical. These are common, day-to-day thought processes that have been stretched out over a period of decades instead of days, because they never got resolved. The only strange thing is that, by the time we get a chance to practice what we rehearsed, we have forgotten how the story started. We are struggling to answer a question we forgot we had even asked: *how do I make things better?*

Children are not deaf-mutes. They feel pain, and they observe pain in others, both physical and emotional. They have no power, and they have a very limited understanding of the motivations and behaviors of the people around them. They do, however, have very creative imaginations. Children try to imagine ways of being, ways of responding, ways of feeling, that would protect themselves and others from the pain they feel.

Now, we don't have to be talking about child abuse, violence or cruelty. Other conditions such as loneliness, depression, mental illness, divorce, estrangement, poverty, substance abuse all create environments in which children might wish to fantasize about the things they might be able to do someday to make things better.

A child who had an alcoholic parent is likely to have fantasized about being able to use the power of love to convince that parent to give up drinking. A child whose mother suffered from abuse, or poverty or depression, surely has fantasies about rescuing that parent and making everything better.

It is impossible for a heart to live with a constellation of needs (spoken or unspoken, acknowledged or hidden) without being able to recognize those needs at a glance.

Do we imagine that our hearts are blind?

Our hearts see more than our eyes.
And then the heart whispers…

As children, we were powerless to change anything, but surely, surely now that we are grown we will be able to meet the need, fill the void, solve the problem and make the hurt go away. Please God, let it be so.

Perhaps you are like me.

I would do anything to have been able to ease my mother's pain, but I couldn't. So I was drawn like a moth to a flame to that *same* pain as reflected in dozens upon dozens of other women's hearts. I found women who were afraid, abandoned, lonely and abused. Each time I hoped that *this* time I could make a difference.

But I never did.

Each person is responsible to God to solve their own problems. We can offer each other love and support and guidance, but we can't fix anyone else. This is attested to by millions upon millions of broken hearts.

Sometimes our desire to fix old hurts is played out in ways that are laughably obvious. If you watch your own patterns, or those of your friends, you may see people being attracted to the same kinds of people over and over again. For example, my mother has red hair, so I tried to date every woman with red hair I met. Other men only date blonds, or skinny over-achievers. Some women only date athletes or men who drive fast cars. It would be funny if it weren't so painful.

Other times, the patterns we are repeating are not so obvious. It took me years to realize that most of the women to whom I was sexually attracted had been sexually abused as children, and most of the women with whom I wanted to be best friends were manic-depressive. This does not mean that they weren't also wonderful people, but it did mean that a good portion of our relationship wasn't about *us* at all. Part of me had one foot in the past, trying to heal the people in my family whom I loved. It wasn't fair to these current relationships, and it didn't change the old ones. I failed them both, and the guilt of that double failure ate me up inside.

Healing *Shame*

Shame leads us into unhealthy relationships.
Shame is what we feel at the end of them.
Shame is what we are taught to feel about ourselves.
Shame is what we beat ourselves up with for our failures.
Shame is what we try to hide from through our acting out.
Shame is what our acting out leads to.

If you are reading this book because you are struggling to control inappropriate behaviors, then shame is probably the dominating force in your life much of the time.

That's OK.

Don't be ashamed.

We can do something to change that.

The first step is to understand what healthy shame is.

The second step is to see how our cultural beliefs cause it to become unhealthy.

The third step is to understand shame spirals.

The fourth step is to stop using shameful behaviors to numb the shame.

There are alternative ways to escape shame that are much more fun than shameful behaviors.

I promise.

What is Shame?

First of all, we need to know what healthy shame is.* Shame is simply an emotional reaction to a flash of self-awareness in which we realize that we are not perfect, that we are, in fact, human. This is a good thing. Being human is a good thing. *Knowing* we are human is a good thing. Knowing that we are not perfect is a *very good thing*.

Shame is like a little alarm that buzzes when we make a mistake. It lets us know that we need to adjust our behavior. Without it, we cannot recognize or learn from mistakes. We cannot become better. Because it is generally an unpleasant sensation, it motivates us to avoid shameful situations and behaviors.

So, if healthy shame is a good thing, how does it become unhealthy? Shame becomes toxic when we combine it with two unhealthy beliefs that are almost universally accepted by our culture. The first is perfectionism. The second is black-and-white thinking (also known as *all-or-nothing* thinking).

When we do anything, what we are really doing is making a choice. Most choices are rarely earth-shattering; they simply involve an attempt to balance competing goals. When added together over the course of our lives, however, these choices define who we are and create our legacy. When we feel a twinge of shame, it is simply telling us that the decision we just made could have been better. This is a good thing, because it allows us to either change our decision, or make a different one in the future.

Our shame alarm is designed to sound only if the difference between our two choices is moderately significant. Like a smoke detector, it is designed to ignore household dust or even Chinese stir-fry cooking. It only sounds if we are in danger of doing something spiritually unhealthy.

---

*Note: different therapeutic systems use the words guilt and shame differently. Since there are no universally-accepted definitions, if you use the ones I give here, the rest of the book will make more sense.

If, however, we are perfectionists, then our internal alarm is set for zero tolerance. Since perfection is impossible, our shame response gets stuck in the on position permanently.

Likewise, black-and-white thinking — the belief that everything is either right or wrong, good or bad, saved or damned — locks our shame alarm on high volume. It doesn't matter whether we pretend that we are godly or unrepentant, there is always a part of us that knows that we aren't 100% right, so we secretly feel we must be 100% wrong.

While perfectionism tells us that we have to be perfect, black-and-white thinking tells us how dire the consequences of failure will be.

This attitude is reinforced by our culture's dominant religious beliefs. Even if we are not raised Christian, a belief in original sin and heaven and hell is infused into almost every aspect of our culture. As a result, we carry a saved/damned duality deep in our psyches. For centuries, Christianity has taught that we are in need of salvation and deserving of damnation. It has also described a stark, black-and-white division between the forces of good and the forces of evil. The last few decades have seen a shift in some denominations, with even the Pope himself saying that hell is not a place, but a state of being far from God. This is a wonderful realization. Unfortunately, few people have heard this statement, and fewer still have been able to believe it. Two-thousand years of self-loathing and fear of punishment do not disappear from our collective world-view that easily.

Knowing we are forgiven and feeling forgiven are two very different things. When we feel unforgivable we continue to punish ourselves with shame.

The way we perceive right and wrong
affects our ability to heal our shame.

HEALING SHAME

involves letting go of Perfectionism,
Black & White Thinking,
and Shamelessness.

Perfectionist: I should be here

WORST	BEST

Black & White: I have to be
at least here

BAD	GOOD

Black & White Perfectionist:
I have to be at least here

HERE THERE BE DEMONS

The Shameless:
I can't improve, so why try?

GOOD AND BAD ARE ARBITRARY ANYWAY

Healthy Shame:
I would rather be <u>here</u>
than here

WORSE	BETTER

We all know what people do with smoke detectors that have zero tolerance. If it goes off every time we cook a meal, light a candle, or smoke a cigarette, then pretty soon we decide to unplug the battery.

No one can live with a smoke alarm going off in his head every minute. Likewise, no one can be happy when tormented by shame. We have to find a way to escape the buzzing alarm, the flush of embarrassment, the pang of guilt and the wave of regret that we experience when shame comes to dominate our lives.

Given the fact that perfectionism and black-and-white thinking have dominated Western culture for thousands of years, it is understandable that many people have chosen to react to these influences by swinging 180 degrees in the opposite direction. Rather than fixing the shame alarm by developing reasonable personal expectations and learning to appreciate the full spectrum of moral choices, they have tried to simply pull the plug on shame.

They try to fool themselves into thinking that inappropriate behavior is perfectly fine. There are no "rules." Everything is relative and arbitrary. If it feels good, they should be able to do it, and shame is a prudish response to be ignored if at all possible.

Unfortunately, it is NOT possible to ignore shame. Unhealthy shame is unhealthy, but to have NO shame leads us to behave in ways that are not becoming to our nobility as reflections of the attributes and virtues of God. No matter what our heads tell us, our hearts know something different. Because of this, we need to find a way to turn off the screaming shame siren in our heads while leaving the healthy little warning tingles intact.

One tool for achieving this is to understand shame spirals.

Shame Spirals

My nephew, who is wise beyond his years, posted this on Facebook:

TO DO LIST:

Find a cookie.
Tell yourself that eating the cookie is a bad idea.
Eat the cookie anyway.
Regret eating the cookie.
Deal with guilt by looking for more cookies.

Since our hearts will not allow us to permanently pull the plug on shame, we are left to find other ways to silence the alarm. The world is full of short fixes. Drugs, alcohol, sex, pornography, over-eating, shopping, gambling, television, web-surfing, games, gossip, sleep, and even work can be used to temporarily numb or distract us from our feelings of shame. An over-eater feels great for the 20 minutes it takes to eat a pint of ice cream, and the TV-addict is dead to shame as long as the tube is on.

The problem is that when we stop our numbing behavior, the numbness starts to go away. Eventually, a part of us wakes up to the understanding that the behavior was not good for us.

It doesn't take long before we begin to feel even more gluttonous, horny, lazy, evil or sick than we did before. When this happens, it is even more tempting to start numbing ourselves again. This is how it becomes a shame spiral. The very behavior that numbs the shame also feeds the shame. People who are caught in this spiral are miserable, but are often too ashamed to ask for help.

There are probably almost as many kinds of shame spirals as there are people in the world, but there is one that is more common than most that I would like to use as an illustration before addressing the steps it takes to break one.

Love, Sex and Shame, the Universal Spiral

Humans have a universal need for love. Humans are also created with a biological desire for sex. Love and marriage, love and sex, love and belonging, these are the conscious associations we have between love and sex.

It is tragic, then, that before this sweet and positive association can be planted in our conscious minds, a much less pleasant association has already taken root in our subconscious minds. Before children have the foggiest idea of what the word sex actually means, they absorb the cultural attitude that it is somehow shameful and evil. Body parts, bodily functions, kissing, nakedness, sex, ewww, GROSS! I don't think anyone on the planet can escape the constant and highly-charged association of sex with shame.

Here's the problem. Associations go two ways. If we are constantly bombarded with SEX = SHAME, SEX = SHAME, SEX = SHAME, then it is impossible not to also respond with SHAME = SEX. In other words, if we associate sex with shame, then when something happens to us that causes us to suddenly feel ashamed – even if it is *healthy* shame, our subconscious minds will start thinking about sex. If we *consciously* start thinking about sex at inappropriate times or with inappropriate people, then this can generate even *more* shame.

Now throw love into the mix. We subconsciously associate sex with shame, but we consciously associate it with love. That means that we also associate love with shame. We have a legitimate and natural desire to find love, but because we associate this love with sex, we feel ashamed of our desire for love.

Now consider the fact that love, sex and shame all generate what *should* be unique physical and spiritual sensations. Because love, sex and shame are all tied into knots in our subconscious, the sensations that they generate also associate, interact, overlap and get confused, one with another. When we feel a strong reaction to a person or situation, our conscious mind has no way to decipher the feelings that are washing over it. Is it love, lust, shame, fear, confusion, or a combination of all of them? Which sensation should be exalted, and which should be numbed? Which is a sign from God, and which is a temptation from a lower nature?

Caught in the whirlwind of conflicting emotions, sensations and interpretations, we often choose the wrong course of action, only to realize hours, days, or years later that we zigged when we should have zagged, and what we thought we were pursuing was not what we snagged.

When that happens, then the shame rises to the surface, and the search begins for some way to numb it. Drugs, alcohol, flirtation, sex, sugar, shopping, pornography, gambling, there are dozens of ways to numb shame. If the substance or behavior that numbs the shame is something that can also *cause* shame, then a spiral has begun.

You can see from this that a shame spiral can be started by something *other* than the behavior that keeps it going. In fact, it is likely that it was. For many, the part of the shame spiral that keeps us numb is all that we can see. It becomes the *identified problem* that keeps us distracted from the deeper source of shame that hides behind it. Almost anyone in recovery will tell you that breaking the addiction is only the first step. It is what is *behind* the unhealthy behavior that takes the real work.

But then... maybe I shouldn't have told you that.

If you picked up this innocent looking book thinking that it would give you a quick fix for your identified problem and then let you go right on being the same person, you might not be very happy to learn that that is only the beginning. Before you are through, you may have to change your understanding of *who you are* from the bottom up. Not everyone is ready for that. For any solution to work, however, you have to really *want* to get at the source of your behaviors, or you will sabotage your efforts to change them and you will never get a chance to peek behind the curtain.

Do you *want* to become a happy, healthy, fully-present person? OK, good. Then let's break this shame spiral.

⊗

Breaking the Shame Spiral

In trying to find a way to break this spiral, the cookie analogy might be helpful. It has five steps:

> 1. *Find a cookie.*
> 2. *Tell yourself that eating the cookie is a bad idea.*
> 3. *Eat the cookie anyway.*
> 4. *Regret eating the cookie.*
> 5. *Deal with guilt by looking for more cookies.*

This means that there are multiple points at which you can break the cycle. Most people focus on #3, and they think that if they work harder at #2 then they will break the cycle there. **Ha**. The more intensely you do #2, the more you set yourself up for #4. The whole cycle is designed to maximize shame so that you can justify keeping the cycle going.

What I recommend instead is to reduce the level of shame and guilt so that you aren't motivated to numb them with more acting out.

The way to do this is to:
1. Develop a more mature approach to perfectionism.
2. Be more "present" during the behavior so you can better understand your motivations and the payoff you are getting for continuing it.
3. *Replace* rather than *resist* unhealthy patterns.
4. Utilize a different kind of motivator, one based on your longing for God rather than shame over your mistakes.
5. Learn about and practice virtues, particularly the virtues of honesty, forgiveness and compassion.

While shame spirals involve a circular process of negative reinforcement, spiritual healing is a holistic process of positive reinforcement. Doing a little bit of any one of these things will make it easier to do all of the others. Start anywhere, take baby steps, and the incremental changes will create exponential progress.

※

Transforming Our Perfectionism

The first step in breaking our shame spirals is to deal with our perfectionism. Earlier I explained how perfectionism helps generate shame. Let's review that idea, and then explore how to transform perfectionism into something healthy.

Perfectionism turns every success into a failure. When you try to celebrate, it whispers in your ear that you should have done better. Though I have absolutely no idea of what specific things your personal demons are saying to you, I have a pretty good idea of the general themes of their chorus:

You will never be good enough.

Close to good enough is nowhere *near* good enough – you are either in or out, saved or damned, acceptable or unworthy.

These two closely-related attitudes, perfectionism and black-and-white thinking, pervade our culture and poison our beliefs about ourselves. The difference between them is that perfectionism says that you need to be perfect, but can imagine shades of grey leading up to that perfection. Black-and-white thinking says that there is no grey. If it is not perfect, it must be evil.

Combined, these two attitudes are deadly, and yet they form the foundation of much of our beliefs about ourselves and the world. Once we have acknowledged the damage that they can cause, we are still left with the dilemma of how to escape them. It would be nice if we could just tell ourselves to stop being such perfectionists, and did! Unfortunately, it is not that easy. Perfectionism carries with it a built-in catch-22, a kind of circular logic that is difficult to break away from.

If I need to be perfect, then to acknowledge that this need *itself* is unhealthy would violate my need to be perfect.

Before I can accept that I've been wrong to believe in perfectionism, I have to accept that it is all right to be wrong. But I can't allow myself to be wrong until *after* I accept that it is OK to not be perfect. Aargh! It gets even more complicated.

Some of us are willing to accept that we have been wrong. After all, our shame comes from the fact that we believe we are *not* good enough. But then there is the question of *where we learned* our perfectionism. We did not wake up as infants and decide, "I think that if I am not perfect, I should be ashamed of myself."

No, we were *taught* to feel shame for being imperfect. We were taught by people who wanted us to believe that *they* were always right, because they also feared the shame of imperfection. The people who taught us perfectionism and black-and-white thinking were our parents, teachers and clergy.

Consciously trying to contradict these sources of inner authority can stir up all sorts of emotions, including even more shame. We are betraying people we love, contradicting people we are supposed to respect, and denying the teachings of those who claim to represent God Himself. That's a lot to fight against just to give yourself a little wiggle room in the area of perfection.

The answer to this dilemma, I believe, is that instead of denying perfectionism and labeling black-and-white thinking, *wrong* and a *mistake*, we can *transform* our old attitudes by listening to, respecting and educating them. Instead of doing battle with our inner demons, we can understand where they came from, the purpose they served, and how they can grow into something new.

In short, we can introduce the concept of *appropriate* to our world-view. This allows us to see perfectionism and black-and-white thinking as good, right, useful and *appropriate* for many times, places and situations, while not being helpful here and now.

Perfectionism is *appropriate* in a dangerous and competitive world where small mistakes can cost you your life. Black-and-white thinking is *natural and appropriate* for children who are trying to make sense of the world by clinging to rules and order. It is *understandable* that imperfect church leaders would interpret the perfect teachings of a loving religion based on their own fears and need for rules and order.

But now… *now,* a different, more mature attitude towards life, perfection and God are *more appropriate.* We can thank our parents, thank our leaders, thank the powers of earth and heaven that held civilization together long enough for us to be able to see things differently. And it is with this attitude of openness and forgiveness that we will be *able* to see things differently without sabotaging ourselves with shame and fear over our audacity to think something new.

We will talk about this attitude of openness and forgiveness again in book two, because perfectionism is not the only demon that needs to be stared straight in the eye and lovingly transformed rather than beaten down.

Once we have the right attitude to transform perfectionism, we can replace it with this: The understanding that good and bad, light and dark, are only meaningful when considered in relation to one another.

Life is a process of moving from darker grays to lighter grays. Where we stand is not as important as which direction we are moving in. We are not simply *loving.* We are either *more* or *less* loving than we were yesterday. We should not feel shame for being imperfect. We should only be alarmed if we do something that moves us backwards dramatically. A mature individual is able to recognize options as better and worse, rather than as good and bad. Adults should be able to see the consequences of their choices as reasonable successes or relative failures, rather than wins and losses.

Another important understanding is that God neither expects nor desires perfection. Our mistakes are learning experiences that bring us closer to achieving our spiritual potential. Recognizing that some of our most shameful qualities can be seen as *virtues in the rough* may allow us to love and forgive those aspects of ourselves that we try hardest to hide.

You may have noticed that there is a big difference between what I am describing and both the traditional religious view *and* the newer alternative perspectives.

As I've noted, mainstream religions often see good and evil as opposing forces. This leaves individuals feeling trapped in an internal battle. There is no middle ground, no shades of gray, so every slip from perfection is a fall into hell.

The modern attitude of moral relativism, on the other hand, often dismisses distinctions entirely. Instead of acknowledging the gray area between light and darkness, it ignores darkness entirely, claiming that all actions are equally good because we are the creators of our own reality. This approach is intended to reduce people's sense of shame, but it runs the danger of backfiring. By making no distinctions, it encourages unhealthy, inappropriate behavior. Inappropriate behaviors have real-world consequences that can destroy our lives whether we feel shame over them or not.

What we want is *healthy* shame, not toxic shame or no shame at all. Perhaps another analogy would be helpful: Guilt, shame and fear are like the guide rail in the middle of the track in a kiddie car ride. You can drift a few feet to the right or left and shame will pull you back on track, but if you ignore the scrapes and bumps and drive completely over the rail, it will be really hard to get back in line. The pain, shame and fear that you felt when you veered away from what was right lingers in your memory. You know that to get back on track, you will have to face that shame again. It is easier, sometimes, to drive off into the trackless wilderness than to acknowledge that you are not where you need to be. You will need to lower that barrier by reducing your shame, so that it is not too painful to admit that you've made a wrong turn.

Being Present

The second step in breaking our shame spirals is to focus on being present. Being "present" means that you continue to pay attention to your thoughts, feelings and sensations, monitoring all three — staying in the moment even as you participate in behaviors designed to keep you numb and distracted.

In the early stages of your healing, you might not be able to stop yourself from doing inappropriate things, but you *can* try to stay present before, during, and especially *after* you do something so that you can be open to hints of your true needs and motivations. Find ways to listen to and monitor the negative messages of your inner critic and private demons. If you are going to make mistakes, you might as well milk them for as much information as possible so that you can learn from them.

I once participated in a unique exercise called "The Cocktail Party." At a real cocktail party, people often stand around talking, but rarely actually listen to anyone else. People are sort of strutting back and forth presenting a mask, pretending to be someone they aren't.

In the cocktail party exercise, a dozen people were put in a small circle, with the lights turned down, and were told to let our "limiting characters" have their voice. We walked around for two hours yelling, crying, blaming, shaming, denying, arguing, accusing, and, in essence, letting our inner demons share their fears and concerns. No one listened to anyone else. We were all just props for each other. We would walk by one person and yell at them like they were a parent. Another would be ourselves. Another would be the whole damned world. We said things that we had not allowed ourselves to even acknowledge we had ever thought, and we brought up into the conscious world feelings that had lain hidden for lifetimes.

When we go directly from inappropriate behavior to shame, we close the door to any opportunity to learn from our mistakes. We are too busy shaming our inner motivations to even consider asking them what they are and where they came from. It would be helpful if we could, instead, hold our shame at bay long enough to discover what it is hiding from us.

On the way home from one inappropriate encounter, I allowed my limiting characters the opportunity to hold a mini-cocktail party. I gave voice to my inner critics, and they had a lot to say. "God was going to punish me, I was a criminal, a heart-breaker, an irresponsible male – just like my father. I would catch a disease, I would be blackmailed, I would go broke, everyone would hate me"… and on and on for half an hour.

Wow. So this was what went on in the back of my head every time I did something wrong? No wonder I tried to keep the voices quiet through more numbing behavior. But this time, instead of telling the voices to go away and shut up, I thanked them. "Gee. I never knew you carried so much fear and concern for my well-being. I appreciate the effort you've been going through to try to keep me safe, but, really, let's consider each of these fears and see how likely they all are."

I then went on to calmly and respectfully examine the claims of my inner critic, and integrated them into my conscious awareness. Once these fears had been heard, they no longer felt the need to shout, and they no longer generated intense sensations when they were ignored. That one blast of honesty went a very long way in helping me break my shame cycle.

There are several less intense ways to gain a deeper understanding of your emotional motivations. These include meditation techniques, such as the one described in *The Power of Focusing* by Ann Weiser Cornell, Ph.D. which I recommend very highly. Another tool is the kind of daily writing exercise that Julia Cameron, author of *The Artist's Way*, encourages. Journaling, twelve-step meetings, therapy sessions, or just shaking your fist at the moon and shouting your fears and frustrations out loud can all help loosen up some inner awareness. When you are done, a few moments of prayer can help calm you back down.

You can also simply take some time and calmly communicate with your emotional self through a process I call Internal Consultation.

Consulting with Your Emotions

Internal Consultation is a powerful tool for identifying the message of the sensations that your emotions are generating. It does not require money, tools or even a therapist, though they can often be helpful. If it sounds similar to other techniques you've used, it probably is. It isn't rocket science, but it can certainly take you places.

Here are the basics:

Sit quietly and comfortably.

Close your eyes if you like.

Become aware of your body.

Check for any sensations.

Be open to sensations that you can't put your finger on or give a name. Pay particular attention to the area around your throat, heart, chest and stomach. Check for sensations that might signal stress, like tightness, heaviness, heat, and pain. Also check for sensations that might signal positive reactions like lightness, warmth and calm.

When you become aware of a physical or emotional sensation, don't pounce on it. Approach it as you would a butterfly. Your goal is to give it a name or hear its message, not grab it and shake it.

The meaning of the sensation may not come to you in words, so be open to other forms of communication.

Become aware of your inner vision – your visual imagination.

Check for any images or pictures that might come to you.

Be open to images glimpsed out of the corner of your mind's eye.

Be aware of your inner voice – your inner community.

Check for any voices that would like to be heard.

Be open to random phrases, lines from songs or poems, quiet voices.

If anything comes to you, welcome it. If it has a name, say hello. If you're not sure of its name, ask open-ended questions to find out what it is and what it wants to communicate with you.

This is not an interrogation.

It is similar to what is often referred to as inner-child work, but what you hear won't necessarily be a child. You will want to maintain an attitude of welcome acceptance, curiosity, tenderness, empathy. Often, once you have a sense of what is present, all you will need to do is sit with it comfortably. Its presence is its own message – no more need be said. At other times, you will want to explore what is behind or accompanying a presence.

This process is called internal consultation rather than internal listening because you are trying to create a relationship with this part of you that has something to share. Whatever it has to share is always true – for that part of you – but not necessarily true for all of you. It is important to give it a voice without giving it power over you.

This feeling, sensation, belief, experience or observation deserves to be heard, but you are under no obligation to agree with it. In fact, the whole point of using this process is to uncover feelings and beliefs that have been misunderstood or have led you in unhelpful directions. The goal is not to accept them or reject them, but rather to gently guide them towards understandings that are more mature and consistent with your current vision. This is a process of guidance and education, not coercion.

Often is it enough to just acknowledge a feeling or thought without trying to change it or give it advice. This is because many times the message that a feeling is trying to send is simply, "I'm here!" Simply saying hello to it can release the energy that has been trying to get your attention.

If you've had any experience with working with a good therapist, then you may identify with this scenario. You can be in turmoil all week because of some event or personal interaction. You are sure it is going to take hours to work through with your therapist, but after hearing just a few minutes of your ranting, your therapist says, "It sounds to me like you might be feeling _____." ... And instantly the turmoil is gone. You've been heard. That's all you needed.

When we learn how to do this for ourselves, we can save ourselves a lot of turmoil (and therapy sessions).

I'm reminded of the scene in the movie *It's a Wonderful Life*, in which the child follows George Bailey around pulling on his coattails saying, "Excuse me" at successively higher volume until his father finally turns in exasperation and says, "Excuse you for what?" To which he replies, "I burped."

Like a burp that is not nearly as annoying as the bellowed request to be excused, the fears, transgressions and concerns that generate powerful internal sensations are often of much less significance than the irritation they generate when they are not acknowledged.

Even when the issues are of great importance, the resolution may not require any intervention because the "you" who is uncovering the issue has more internal resources than the "you" who generated the issue. In other words, issues that were buried when you were a child because you didn't have the emotional resources and experience to deal with them are now easy to handle – once they have a name.

Another reason why simply acknowledging a feeling can instantly resolve tension has to do with the nature of emotions themselves. Emotions tell us about the presence or absence of virtues in our lives. Simply naming the emotion can help us understand our situation more clearly and resolve all sorts of inner turmoil.

For example, sadness tells us that we perceive the loss of a source of goodness in our lives. It tells us, "You did have access to this source of virtue; now you don't." In order to hide sadness from ourselves, we must convince ourselves that either A) the thing we have lost isn't really gone, or B) the thing we lost didn't really have any value to us in the first place.

Any time we try to convince ourselves that something we love isn't really valuable, the part of us that loves goodness is going to start screaming at us. It will jump up and down, it will grab hold of our heart, our throat or our stomach and start squeezing.

If we want this tightness to go away, all we have to do is say, "I'm sad about ___." In doing so, we are admitting that we have lost something of value. Once we acknowledge that something has value to us, it is often much easier to accept the fact that it is gone and get on about the business of find-ing some other source of goodness to fill the void. So acknowl-edging sadness can make it go away. It's not magic. It's just dismissing the messenger after the message has been deliv-ered!

If naming an emotion doesn't instantly clarify the nature of the message behind it, you might want to ask any strong emotional sensation what virtue or attribute it is responding to. There are, of course, some sensations that will require more than a name. They may be associated with traumatic experi-ences, major life events, long-term perspectives, or family sys-tems. It is OK to call a feeling "something" and just sit with it to see what it has to share.

When you are done, say *thank you* and ask if it is all right to move on.

Then write down whatever of value you can put into words while the new awareness is still fresh. Creating an objective record of your internal experiences will help make them real and give you something to refer back to if your new-found understandings start to get cloudy.

Some additional tips and tricks:

The goal of internal consultation is to receive the message and honor the messenger, not become overwhelmed by ei-ther of them. The advantage of naming a sensation or an aware-ness is that it establishes a distinction between you and it. It creates a safe distance between you.

Don't eat or drink while practicing internal consultation. Physical sensations often serve double-duty. Physical hunger and spiritual emptiness, for example, can feel the same. Eat-ing can interfere with an awareness of emotional cues.

I often visualize my mind as a rock tumbler. I toss an idea or word or feeling in and just let it roll around for a while until something tumbles forward and makes a connection.

46   Justice Saint Rain

Replacing Old Patterns

The third step in breaking shame spirals is to focus on *replacing* old patterns rather than resisting them. One of the great truisms of life is that nature abhors a vacuum. That is just as true of our spiritual lives as it is of the material universe. When we find ourselves caught up in a self-destructive spiral of inappropriate activity, our first impulse is to try to *stop* ourselves from engaging in that activity.

This approach is doomed to failure.

Every time.

Why?

Because negative behavior is caused by a need, a lack of some positive quality. One cannot remove a lack. One can only fill a need. We cannot remove darkness, we can only add light.

There is another reason. The soul hungers for sensation. Shame, fear and anger may be poor substitutes for love, peace and joy, but they are better than no sensations at all. To have no sensations feels like death.

> *She said move me, move me. I'm locked up inside.*
> *But I didn't understand her, though God knows I tried.*
> *She said make me angry, or just make me cry.*
> *But no more grey mornings. I think I'd rather die.*
> — James Taylor

Think about it. The only way we know that we are alive is by our senses. If we could not see, hear, touch taste or feel, how would we know we were alive? People placed in sensory deprivation tanks for too long start to lose their sense of identity. If the body needs physical sensations to feel alive, would not the soul need them too?

When we tell ourselves that we need to stop doing the things we are currently doing, what our soul hears is that we are going to stop doing the things that make it feel alive. To the subconscious, this sounds like a kind of spiritual death. It is frightening. Just as depressed people might cut themselves just to prove that they can still feel, the soul would rather continue experiencing painful emotional sensations than to feel nothing at all.

We *need* these sensations to feel alive, and will do almost anything to make them continue. That is one reason why we sabotage our own efforts at stopping our self-destructive behavior. It is better to self-destruct than to fade into oblivion.

This is why we can't just stop what we are doing. To change a behavior, we must replace it with a healthier behavior. To do that, we need to understand *why* we have chosen the behaviors we have, and find a new source of motivation that will urge us towards healthier behaviors.

⌘

Changing our Motivation

In order to be successful in adopting new, healthy behaviors, we need to look at what motivates those behaviors in the first place. So the fourth step in breaking our shame spiral is to change our source of motivation. To do that, it would help to understand exactly how shame, a negative emotion, manages to motivate so much of our behavior.

As I've explained, a little bit of healthy shame acts as a warning signal when we are about to make an unhealthy decision. It motivates us to stop and reconsider what we are about to do, or what we have just done. If a little bit of shame can stop us from making a small mistake, then wouldn't it make sense that a lot of shame would motivate us to avoid making a big mistake? No. Not after it becomes toxic.

Here is why.

If we only feel shame once in a while, then we know that we can make it go away by making a better decision. The ability to turn off the unpleasant sensation is an effective motivator. But if shame is with us all of the time, then we don't feel that we have the ability to turn it off. As our feelings of shame increase, we are motivated, instead, to *manage* our shame by doing one of several things:

Distract ourselves from it
Numb ourselves to its effect
Redefine it as something positive
Adopt it as part of our identity

When this happens, shame actually becomes the motivation for doing the very things that it was intended to discourage. That means that using shame to try to *stop* ourselves from the behaviors that are part of our shame spiral is counterproductive. Let me give you some examples:

Would you rather feel loved or shamed? Hmmm. So, if a person whispers in your ear that they love you and want to have sex with you, but your shame meter is going haywire telling you that this is a bad idea, which are you going to want to listen to? You are probably going to distract yourself from the shame by focusing on the promise of love. When given the choice, love (even imitation love) always wins. This is why shaming youth into abstinence doesn't work.

But it is not just sex that people can use as a distraction. There are lots of strong physical and emotional sensations that we can use to distract ourselves from shame's warning signals – lust, excitement, loud music, dangerous activities. These are sensations that overpower the sensation of shame and distract us from its warning signal. They don't necessarily have to be unhealthy activities, though many are, they just have to generate strong sensations. When we ask ourselves "why am I doing this?" we think it is because we are attracted to the strong sensations the activity generates. We don't realize that the *real* motivation is the need to distract ourselves from shame.

When shame becomes too strong to overpower, then the next step is to numb it. Some distracting activities can also numb shame, but usually numbing activities are more passive and serve to shut down our feelings or disconnect us from our bodies. Eating, watching TV, gambling, shopping, working, masturbation, loveless sex – these can all numb a little shame. As the shame increases, the need to numb also increases and so these behaviors can become obsessive.

As our cookie analogy illustrates, if one cookie numbs a little shame, it can take a whole box of cookies to numb a lot of shame. From the outside, the motivation appears to be a love of cookies, but beneath it all, the real motivation is the numbing of shame. Shaming ourselves for these behaviors just increases them, while a healthier motivation will lead us to healthier behaviors.

What happens if shame breaks through our efforts at distraction and numbing behavior? People can do what I did, and redefine the sensation of shame as feelings of love, or feelings of power, or feelings of excitement. By misidentifying shame as something good, it can lead us into all sorts of unhealthy behavior. It motivates us to do the exact opposite of what is best for us. For me, this happened when I faced an unexpected and strong source of shame that wasn't part of my usual shame spiral, but it can happen at any time.

The last stage in this progression is when we realize that we are *enjoying* the sensation of shame, and we give up trying to fool ourselves into believing that what we are doing is healthy. Shame becomes the central core of our identity. We behave in shameful ways because we see ourselves as shameful beings. We are "bad to the bone" or think of ourselves as outlaws or loners or wild ones, or simply broken. Doing shameful things is how we remain true to ourselves. The flashing red light of shame is no longer a warning signal, it is our destination.

If you have been told all of your life that you are sinful, evil, and deserving of punishment, and if you have given up hope of ever getting into heaven, then shame becomes a mark of honor, and self-destruction is a way of life. This does not have to be a conscious awareness. Many of us wear the mask of respectability while secretly believing that we are beyond redemption. Our subconscious is filled with the noise of inner demons and critics that only the numbing sensation of shame can drown out. Shame is our guiding light and motivating force.

These are just four of the ways in which we can allow our choices in life to be guided by shame. They also describe why shame is *not* the source of motivation we should choose for ourselves. But is there an *alternative* to shame that is strong enough to get us out of bed in the morning?

Yep. And it is a lot more fun.

☒

Joy and Longing as Motivators

If shame makes a bad motivator, perhaps the opposite of shame would be a good motivator. At its essence, shame is the sensation of suddenly moving away from God, or away from your spiritual potential. It is the sensation of slipping backwards, or falling a short distance, as though you unexpectedly stepped off of a curb. The opposite of falling away is flying toward. This moving towards God and our highest potential is experienced as joy. As Teilhard de Chardin said, *"Joy is the infallible sign of the presence of God."* When we strengthen our virtues, accomplish something noble, and grow closer to God, our hearts take flight.

In the next few pages I will be explaining how we can replace shame with joy by changing our focus from pursuing positive physical sensations to experiencing positive spiritual sensations.

❈

Physical Sensations Vs. Spiritual Sensations

Certainly, the concept of replacing unhealthy behavior with healthy behavior isn't new. People who are trying to diet don't just stop eating. They try to replace unhealthy food with the kind that will provide nourishment. They think of unhealthy food as bad and try to find the opposite of bad food to eat.

Likewise, people who are in unhealthy relationships will try to find the opposite of an unhealthy relationship in order to fill the holes in their lives. The problem is that people don't understand what it really means to do the opposite of what they are currently doing.

You see, the opposite of black, for example, isn't white. They are both visual sensations. They have more in common than almost any two random words in the dictionary. The opposite of black is God. Black is a physical sensory experience. God is a spiritual reality beyond sensation.

Likewise, the opposite of eating is not dieting—they are both ways of relating to food; they keep the mind focused on *food*.

The opposite of eating is *God*.

The opposite of *drinking* is God.

The opposite of *drugs* is God.

The opposite of *promiscuity* is God.

The opposite of *sickness* is God.

The opposite of *any* physical substance, experience or activity that draws our spirits away from God — is God.

So the cure for *all* of our ills… is *God*.

Focusing our attention on the names and attributes of God draws our hearts and minds away from the world of limitations into a world where perfections are infinite and our capacity for growth is unlimited. Turning towards God is not a process in which we beg God, over and over again, to change our behavior for us – concentrating our thoughts on what we don't want to do and hoping that God is strong enough to stop us. It is a way of turning our attention to a spiritual realm where our addictive behaviors simply do not exist — and therefore cannot take hold of us.

This is why, instead of trying to tell you how to *stop* getting into unhealthy relationships or how to *overcome* compulsive behaviors, the rest of this book - and its sequels - will try to direct your attention in a completely different direction, one focused on developing positive spiritual qualities rather than overcoming negative behaviors. We do this by focusing on *spiritual* sensations rather than physical ones.

Emotions as Spiritual *Perception*

I've mentioned several aspects of this idea since the beginning of this book, but now I want to explain it in detail because it really is one of the keys to achieving spiritual growth.

Emotions are spiritual sensations that tell us about the presence of virtues in our lives. These virtues are the attributes of God that are present in the world around and within us.

Emotions provide the spiritual eyes and ears with which to perceive the qualities of God in the world. When we perceive them, our hearts respond. When we experience their absence, our hearts are troubled.

Put another way, we could say that as physical beings, we need to be able to perceive and respond to our physical environment. Our physical senses allow us to do that.

As *spiritual* beings, we need to be able to perceive and respond to our *spiritual* environment. Our *emotions* allow us to do *that*.

Just as our physical senses communicate with our minds to tell us what is going on around us, our spiritual senses – our emotions – communicate with both our minds and our bodies to prepare us to respond to our spiritual surroundings. Our emotions generate a physical response. They *also* create spiritual feelings that are *more* than just physical.

Up to this point, I've focused on how these sensations can be misinterpreted and lead us astray. Now I would like to focus on how emotions, *when accurately identified as signals of the presence of virtues,* can generate a whole host of wonderful, ecstatic, and immensely satisfying physical and spiritual sensations.

I know, we don't usually think of emotions, let alone *virtues* as the source of wonderful sensations. We usually think of sensations in terms of *physical* pleasures. But our spiritual sensations are even more rich and varied than our physical ones.

When we think of *physical* sensations, for example, we start with our five senses, then combine them in an infinite variety of ways using an infinite number of sources of stimulation. We can't imagine ever feeling everything there is to feel, tasting everything there is to taste, seeing every kind of beauty there is to behold, or even experiencing every kind of sexual pleasure possible.

When we think of our emotions, however, we often limit our thinking to the six that most researchers acknowledge – happiness, sadness, anger, fear, lust and disgust. With only one pleasant, four unpleasant and one very confusing feeling in our emotional vocabulary, it is difficult to imagine our emotional lives ever being able to compete with the physical world as a source of pleasure.

> But there are more than six emotions.
> Emotions are sensations that tell us about the presence of
>   the attributes of God.
> Every attribute, every virtue, can generate a different
>   sensation.
> And the attributes of God are infinite.
> Plus they can be *combined* in an infinite number of ways.
> And the experience of each of those virtues *feels good.*
>
> Misinterpreting, ignoring and denying the sensations
>   that are associated with these virtues *feels bad.*

Trying to bend, push and squeeze the vast array of emotional sensations we experience into six cramped and rigid emotional boxes diminishes the good, exaggerates the bad, and impoverishes us spiritually.

It is very difficult to process an emotional sensation that we don't have a word for. As a result, we try to redefine our experiences to match the emotions that we have a name for.

That is why we redefine shame as lust or love. That is why pity becomes love, or excitement becomes fear, or depression becomes sadness, or ecstasy is reduced to simple happiness.

I often wonder about how people who speak Spanish deal with loneliness, because in Spanish, they can only say, "solo y triste" which means "alone and sad." There is no word for that distinct feeling of being surrounded by people but still feeling lonely. This is the dilemma that all of us face every day when we experience sensations that simply don't fit the emotional labels we've been given. What do we do with them? How do we resolve them? If emotional sensations are messengers, how do we respond to messages that are written in bright red letters, but in a language we don't understand?

⚯

What's in a name?

Our ability to give a name to our emotional response to virtues is not just an exercise in semantics, it is an exercise in identification and knowledge. To name something gives us a kind of power over it. Being able to distinguish between related virtues and related emotions allows us to feel them both, understand them both, strive for them both.

It is important, for example, to understand the difference between the feelings of love, lust, need and pity. If we do not, then our relationships will never be honest.

Even more crucial, our ability to accurately name an emotional sensation gives us an invaluable clue as to the virtue that is involved.

In spite of the fact that most people do not think of emotions in terms of virtues, the vast majority of the virtues that humans strive to acquire *share the name* of the emotion or feeling that they generate.

For example, a kind person feels kindness. A patient person feels patience. A courageous person feels courage, and a compassionate person feels compassion. We feel grateful, happy, joyful, generous, pure, strong, noble, faithful, honest, and friendly.

Look at this list:

Compassion	Grace	Nobility
Confidence	Gratitude	Optimism
Contentment	Happiness	Patience
Courage	Hope	Peace
Creative	Honesty	Perseverance
Determination	Humility	Radiance
Empathy	Initiative	Resilience
Enthusiasm	Integrity	Respect
Faith	Joy	Reverence
Forgiveness	Kindness	Serenity
Friendship	Love	Strength
Generosity	Loyalty	Wonder
Gentleness	Modesty	

Is this a list of virtues, or a list of emotions?

I found these words online in separate lists of each, so the answer is *both*.

When displayed like this, the relationship between virtues and emotions is embarrassingly obvious, and yet few people have noticed. Perhaps it is because, though we have all felt these things, they don't show up on the standard list of six emotions. The feelings aren't overwhelming, and they don't set off physical alarms. They don't start wars, but they *do* inspire discoveries, build communities, connect hearts and add meaning to our lives.

So is it really fair to call these emotions? Do we really *feel* them in our hearts?

Well, consider the exceptions: Have you ever performed a generous act without feeling generous? Of course you have. We often leave a tip, provide a service or give a gift without *feeling* particularly good about it. We do it from a sense of obligation. In those cases, we are *not* feeling generous because we are not actually manifesting the *virtue* of generosity.

Other times, however, we *do* feel an internal desire to give freely of ourselves and our possessions. The fact that we can tell the difference between the two feelings even though the outward expressions are the same proves that the sensations are associated with the virtue rather than the material action.

Gratitude is another virtue that generates strong sensations when it is sincere, and none when it is forced. Here is a great description of this:

"Thankfulness is of various kinds. There is a verbal thanksgiving which is confined to a mere utterance of gratitude. This is of no importance because perchance the tongue may give thanks while the heart is unaware of it. Many who offer thanks to God are of this type, their spirits and hearts unconscious of thanksgiving. This is mere usage, just as when we meet, receive a gift and say thank you, speaking the words without significance. One may say thank you a thousand times while the heart remains thankless, ungrateful. Therefore, mere verbal thanksgiving is without effect. But real thankfulness is a cordial giving of thanks from the heart. When man in response to the favors of God manifests susceptibilities of conscience, the heart is happy, the spirit is exhilarated. These spiritual susceptibilities are ideal thanksgiving."   'Abdu'l-Bahá*

So expressing gratitude makes the heart happy. Remember that. I will mention it again in the section about happiness research.

Look at the list again. Pick any one virtue at random, then roll that word around in your heart. Try to *feel* what it is like to experience that virtue. Hold onto it for a few moments, then pick another word. Can you feel a shift in energy as you move from one word to another?

When you imagine yourself feeling forgiveness, for example, does it feel different from feeling wonder? Do some of these words resonate strongly with you? Do you resist others? Isn't it interesting that simply *reading* the name of a virtue can have an effect on you? Imagine how *receiving* one of these virtues might feel, or, better yet, *living* one of them.

What an amazing array of emotional sensations this list represents!

---

*'Abdu'l-Bahá, *The Promulgation of Universal Peace*, p. 236

When you make an effort to replace old, unhealthy patterns with new, healthy ones, *this* is what you have to look forward to. Each of these virtues (and hundreds more) represent a change in behavior that will improve the quality of your life, generate positive spiritual sensations, and, because our spiritual and physical emotions are so closely linked, will make you feel better physically as well.

With all of these benefits going for them, why isn't everyone in the world rushing to experience the joys associated with experiencing virtues? Why isn't honesty and kindness as popular as beer and sex?

❀

The Down Side of Virtues

There are, of course, lots of reasons why virtues are not as popular as vices. Since you've read this far, however, I have to assume that you are at least open to the idea that virtues are good. Why, then, do you and I have such a difficult time focusing on virtues? If they really are as much fun as I say, it should be easy!

The problem is that in order to be open to the spiritual sensations associated with virtues, we must also be open to the sensations associated with their *absence*. Remember, emotions tell us about the presence or *absence* of a virtue.

Take another look at the list above. How often do you experience any of these virtues in your daily life?

You are a noble, radiant child of God. How often are you treated that way? As a child, you deserved to be cherished and celebrated. As a youth, you deserved to have your creativity unleashed and your enthusiasm appreciated. As an adult, you deserve respect and to be dealt with honestly. We live in an amazing world that should radiate reverence and joy.

In order to acknowledge that we long for these virtues; to even begin to look for them and try to identify them in our personal interactions, we have to admit that our lives are mostly devoid of them.

And that really *really* hurts.

A Story of Longing

One evening I went to hear a gospel choir concert at the Madame Walker Theater in downtown Indianapolis. I went because a Bahá'í choir had been asked to participate along with the choirs of half a dozen local black churches. I went expecting to hear good music. I didn't go expecting to be swept out to sea.

When the music started for the first piece, there were no choirs on stage, only a single director, but as he raised his arms towards the audience, almost a quarter of the room rose as one and lifted their voices up towards heaven in a wave of sound like nothing I had ever experienced in my life.

It was not just that I was surrounded by beautiful voices on all four sides. It was not just that the music was so full of life that you could almost feel the heart beat of the Holy Spirit. It was the ineffable blend of joy, praise, gratitude, reverence, and complete abandon that made me feel as though I had died and gone to heaven.

You see, I'm a white boy from a Lutheran background, and we just don't get that intimate with God. We praise God, all right, but with a slap on the back, not a full-body-contact embrace.

When my heart perceived the possibility of this level of spiritual expression, it experienced a brilliant flash of pure joy — and then immediately recognized its total absence in the rest of my daily life, and I began to weep uncontrollably.

Longing — deep, profound, personal, inconsolable. I believe that this is one of the main reasons why we are willing to limit ourselves to the five or six basic emotions. As soon as our hearts recognize something new, something transcendent, something beyond our normal daily experience, they leap for joy, then crash against the wall of longing.

To acknowledge that kindness exists is to face the overwhelming lack of it in our daily interactions. To experience generosity is to recognize the ubiquity of selfishness in our interactions. To receive grace is to become aware of how few things we have forgiven ourselves and others for. And so we almost instantaneously slide from the joyful sensation of the virtue to the painful awareness of its general absence and a deep longing for its return.

How many times have you been watching some silly movie, a sappy commercial on TV, or even listening to a country & western song, when a character says or does something kind, loving or generous *without a personal payoff* and suddenly you get a lump in your throat? I have to admit, I'm an easy touch. But what interests me is not that I am moved by sweetness, but how quickly my sensation flips from the joy of recognizing a virtue to the pain of that lump. That lump is longing, and it is the fear and embarrassment of experiencing that pain that prevents many of us from seeking out more encounters with divine virtues.

Usually, when I write books and booklets, I focus on the good stuff – how wonderful it is to develop our virtues, and how positive the sensations are when we learn how to be loving and kind and honest and forgiving.

But this isn't that kind of book.

It wouldn't be fair of me to ask things of someone who is struggling with personal issues and pretend that resolving them will be sweet and easy. It won't be.

As I said, we can't open ourselves up to the joys of Divine virtues without simultaneously opening ourselves up to their absence in our lives. And that absence isn't just today's absence. When we realize what we are missing now, we also realize what we've been missing for our entire lives.

There may be a hole in your heart that should have been filled with kindness. There may be a hole in your heart that should contain idealism. For every virtue that you come to fall in love with, there is likely to be a big empty space waiting for it. It hurts. It is supposed to hurt. That's how you know that something is missing. And it is good to take some time to grieve all that you deserved but didn't get. Acknowledge the loss. Understand that it may be appropriate to feel anger.

But it's very important to remember this: the sensation is just a messenger. The sensation tells you that there is something valuable that is missing in your life, but more importantly, it is telling you that you are longing for something that you don't have. That longing can either be pointed backwards into the past, or turned around and pointed towards the future.

This book is part of a trilogy called **Love, Lust and the Longing for God**. Longing tells you that you really, really want something. That is a very good thing.

The stronger your longing, the more energy and motivation you have to go out and get all of the kindness and idealism and enthusiasm you can grab. There is no limit. Your heart has infinite potential for virtue, and God has an infinite supply.

The more you are motivated by longing, the less you will be motivated by shame, and the less attraction you will feel towards old behavior patterns.

Understand, though, that this is not a one-step process. Most people do not look at their life and say, "Gee, I didn't have much experience with positive virtues in my life, but that's OK. I'll fill up all my empty spaces with virtues and go have a happy life!"

Life is a process of uncovering and discovering. Sometimes a painful emotion or memory will point us towards a virtue that we need to develop, while other times our love for a virtue will shed light on our personal history. We grieve, we learn, we grow, we rejoice, then we grieve again.

Dealing with what is missing

Let's look again at the list of emotions that most scientists study: happiness, sadness, lust, anger, fear and disgust.

We can now say that happiness is a catch-all name for the positive sensations we experience when we become aware of any virtues in our lives. When we experience kindness, beauty, creativity, harmony, friendship, generosity, etc. it feels good, and we say that we are happy. You can, in fact, find entire books that claim that the secret of true happiness is one or another of these specific virtues. But the truth is, happiness comes from all of them, and hundreds more. Happiness comes from feeling close to God when we find signs of God around us. Since God is everywhere all the time, we should all be happy most of the time. It is our inability to *recognize* God's virtues in each moment of our lives that allows happiness to elude us.

The nature of sadness, then, is equally obvious. It is a catch-all word to describe how we feel when we search for God's virtues and cannot find them – when something or someone who used to express those virtues is no longer available to us, or when the weight of the world's coarseness gets us down.

Lust, as we've explored in detail, is the coarse physical side of the virtue of love. Love is the heart's attraction to the attributes of God in the world. Happiness tells us we are surrounded by virtues. Sadness tells us that they are absent, and love motivates us to go find more of them.

Love is attraction to virtue, while lust is simply the attraction of one body towards another body. It is, however, easier to measure, so it is the one that science can study and make pronouncements on. With both science and our culture focusing on the physical aspect of this virtue, the meaning of love has been debased.

So what about the other three – anger, fear and disgust? These sensations tell us that what is missing is one of the three most important virtues that we need to survive – both physically and spiritually: Justice, Security and Purity.

Anger tells us that we don't think we are being treated with fairness and justice. Some acts of injustice require an immediate physical response (fight or flight) which is why our bodies react so strongly to this perception. But many acts of injustice require a more measured, thoughtful response. This leaves our bodies all fired up with no place to go. If we understand what we are responding to, we can walk our hearts and bodies back out of the sensation of anger – by changing our perception of the event, resolving the cause of the injustice, or forgiving it and moving on.

If we *don't* understand anger's role as a messenger and cling, instead, to the sensation, then we can carry this extra (negative) energy around for hours, days, or a lifetime. If you find yourself being angry much of the time, then chances are that you faced a lot of injustice in your life that never got resolved. What is missing in your life is a sense that the universe is fair and that God is just and on your side. The virtues that will reduce anger are justice, patience, faith, forgiveness, serenity and compassion, among others.*

Fear tells us that we do not feel safe – either physically or spiritually. Now, we do not often think of safety as a virtue, let alone an attribute of God, and yet scriptures such as these remind us that safety, security and strength are, indeed, qualities of God that we have a right to long for and attain:

"The Lord is my shepherd. I shall not want."

"He only is my rock and my salvation: he is my defense; I shall not be moved."

"My love is My stronghold; he that entereth therein is safe and secure...."

To feel physically safe means that we are confident that our bodies are not going to be attacked or harmed and that our material needs will be met. To feel *spiritually* safe means that our *identities as children of God* are not subject to attack and that our spiritual potential will be allowed to blossom. If we grew up with criticism, nit-picking, ridicule, shame, abandonment, minimization of our accomplishment or our feelings, and, of course, rage, then we lived in a constant state of fear for our spiritual well-being.

The virtues that were missing – the ones that will eliminate the fear – include self-acceptance, security, confidence, personal boundaries, trust in God, detachment, courage and strength, along with many others.

Disgust tells us that something is impure or unhealthy. Physically, we are disgusted by rotten food, feces, dead animals and other things that our bodies tell us we should step away from. Spiritually, we are disgusted by actions and attitudes that we sense would degrade us, or sully us even by association. There are things that our minds and hearts do not need to see or experience. Some people lack positive virtues, while others actively pursue behaviors that harm themselves and others. We have pity on the first, but we are disgusted by the second.

Forgiveness is covered in depth in book 2

Disgust is a legitimate and helpful response that protects us from exposure to harmful experiences, but it can be distorted in two ways. First, it is a sensation, and people who are numb to positive sensations will sometimes choose negative sensations rather than feel completely dead. That's why you will find plenty of television shows and movies that cash in on people's willingness to settle for fear, ridicule, injustice and disgust as a form of entertainment rather than seek out something spiritually uplifting.

Second, if people express disgust for *who we are as people*, as though our very existence makes the world a dirtier place, then we will internalize this attitude as shame.

This was a quick description of just the six emotions that science tends to study. There are obviously hundreds of different virtues, and therefore twice that many emotions – one for each virtue's presence, and one for its absence.

Just as each virtue feels different, the absence of each virtue feels different, as well. So, for example, as *freedom* and *independence* feel different, so do *control* and *manipulation*. When we name our feelings, we are better able to name the virtues that will heal them.

On the next page is a chart with just a few examples of virtues and the emotions they might generate when they are either present or absent.

Each negative emotion gives us a hint of what is missing in our lives. By combining this awareness with the exercise of internal consultation, we can practice a kind of spiritual archeology. Just as fossils are made when hard rock fills in the spaces where soft tissue used to be, painful emotions fill in the spaces where we were most vulnerable. When we find ancient emotions set in stone in our hearts, we can use them to piece together a picture of what might have been missing in our lives. As we discover what is missing, we gain the ability to heal its absence. This is the essence of what it means to consciously engage in spiritual healing.

The virtue	What we feel when it is present or expressed	What we feel when it is absent or removed
Security	serenity, peace	fear
Justice / fairness	satisfaction	anger
Purity	clean	disgust
Strength/competence	confident	helpless/incompetent
All virtues	joy/happiness	sorrow/loss
Connectedness	friendship/belonging	loneliness/isolation
Creativity	creative/alive	passive/apathetic
Integrity	noble/worthy	shame/unworthy
Patience	patient/calm	impatient/agitated
Trust	trustworthy	paranoid
Faith	assured	adrift/anxious
Generosity	generous/open	greedy/selfish

The essence of the healing process is this:

> To uncover a feeling or a memory that points to a
>   virtue that was absent in our lives.
> To acknowledge that absence.
> To grieve that absence.
> Then to foster the longing for that virtue,
>   even if it causes pain.
> Then to create that virtue in our current lives.

This way of looking at what we are doing changes our whole way of thinking. By relating the healing process to virtues, we transform it from a shame-based escape from our failures to the noble enterprise of moving towards God. Our shame came from the belief that *we must not have deserved* what we didn't receive. The holes in our lives were seen as flaws in our character rather than virtues that we were never shown. As we heal our shame, we reclaim our right to strive to develop all of the strengths that we were denied as children.

Shifting our perception of what we are trying to accomplish from "healing an illness" to "developing our divine virtues" brings our efforts into the realm of the sacred. It sets our sights, not on our past, but on our future.

❀

Developing Virtues in our Lives

We heal ourselves – and grow spiritually – by filling the empty places in our lives with Divine virtues. There are two ways to do this. We can surround ourselves with people and experiences that reflect those virtues, or we can express those virtues *ourselves* in our relationship with ourselves and with others.

We would all like to fill our lives with kind, loving, supportive people, but if that were *easy*, I wouldn't be writing this book. Since the only person's virtues we have any control over at all is our own, the most reliable way to fill our lives with virtue is by practicing them ourselves.

It might seem unfair that after living so long without other people showing us the kindness, respect and patience we deserve, we should immediately be expected to try to practice these virtues ourselves instead of finding the "right" person to give us what we need. Yet it is absolutely fair.

Anyone who can show you kindness or understanding or support can also turn around and take it away. But if *you* develop your own capacity to express these virtues, then they will be with you always. You can show them to yourself, or you can offer them to other people, and no one will ever be able to take them away from you. The positive sensations you get from being a kind person, or a patient person, or a forgiving person, will never be conditioned on anyone else. They are yours forever.

This is not as difficult as it may seem. Remember, we are born with a longing for God, and that longing is expressed in our attraction to Divine virtues. The more we understand virtues – define them, visualize them in practice, understand their long-term benefits, experience the sensations they generate – the more we will long for them.

❀

Understanding Virtues

*Virtues are the light of the Divine
reflected in the human heart.*

At first glance, this spiritual definition would not seem to have very much practical application. With deeper reflection, however, this metaphor offers a host of useful insights.

First of all, it reminds us that, like sunlight on a mirror, virtues come from a higher source that is both infinite and eternal. We don't need to be perfect in order to reflect these perfect qualities, all we have to do is point ourselves in the right direction and clean the dust off of our hearts.

Reflecting the light of the sun makes us brilliant, radiant, full of light and life, but that is not all it does. Sunlight is the originating source of virtually all energy – and therefore all physical life – on earth. Likewise, virtues are the source of our spiritual life.

While at first we notice the sun's light, we quickly begin to appreciate its heat as well. In time, we realize that white light is the source of all color in the world. When we really start to explore, we discover that sunlight contains infrared, ultraviolet, radio, x-ray, microwave, and an entire spectrum of energy that can be harnessed to accomplish amazing things.

Likewise, virtues start out as the idea of "being good," but as we explore all of their nuances, we realize that virtues are what allow us to do everything we do. They are the energy that powers our spiritual existence. Virtues are not one thing, nor are they a collection of many separate things, but like the rays of the sun, they express a full spectrum of capacities, behaviors, energies and attractions. Exploring all of their potential is, in the words of a Sufi poet, *"the science of the love of God."*

Other observations we can make from this metaphor are that:

A mirror allows us to reflect the light of the sun into dark places and illumine them. Reflecting virtues illumines the dark areas of our lives.

We are naturally drawn to heat and light, and enjoy diversity of color. Likewise, we are drawn to virtues and enjoy people who express a wide range of them.

We can reflect, experience and enjoy the bounties of the radiant Sun, even though we can never touch the sun itself and may never understand how or why it shines the way it does. Likewise, we don't have to *understand* or even *believe* in God in order to benefit from the qualities we were given. The sun will shine on us, even if we never look up in awe and wonder.

While I obviously love the metaphor of virtues as light reflected in our hearts, there are other analogies that also offer insights. For example:

We can think of virtues as spiritual food that gives us the energy we need to accomplish our goals. In fact, the Bible calls the virtues of love, joy, peace, longsuffering, gentleness, goodness, faith, meekness and temperance the "fruits of the spirit." The term "fruit" can be understood both as spiritual food and as the reward of a spiritual life.

We can think of virtues as our spiritual arms and legs, which allow us to work and serve. When we think of our physical qualities, we include our bodies, our organs and our senses – all of those things that allow us to function in the physical world. Our spiritual qualities are our virtues, combined with our minds and our will. Our virtues are all of the capacities that allow us to function in the world of the spirit.

We can think of virtues as tools in our personal toolbox. The more familiar we are with what tools we have access to, the more likely we are to choose the right one for the job and build the life we want.

Other things it is helpful to know about virtues are:

Practicing virtues is a gift we give ourselves. It is not a sacrifice we make for others. Not only do virtues feel good, but they improve the quality of our lives. Having patience, for example, does not mean that we spend more time waiting for things to happen, it means that we enjoy the time we spend waiting, rather than being frustrated. (The wait will be just as long either way).

Virtues inform and guide our decision-making process. Our minds make decisions and our Will spurs us to action, but our virtues – and the emotions they evoke – set our priorities. The more we love what is good, the easier it is to do what is good.

Virtues need to be in balance with one another. Courage without prudence is recklessness. Honesty without tact becomes hurtful. Almost any virtue, without moderation, becomes a vice.

Our culture often values the wrong qualities. The ability to play guitar, shoot baskets or make money are not spiritual virtues, though the virtues of perseverance, focus and cooperation might make them more attainable.

Virtues are known by many names. When educators and psychologists talk about non-cognitive skills, good character and signature strengths, they are really talking about virtues, but they are ignoring where those virtues come from. By ignoring the spiritual nature of virtues, they loose access to much of their power, inspiration and meaning. That *doesn't* mean that the research is invalid, only that it is incomplete. You and I can use their research to validate the importance of virtues, then look for the deeper meaning behind it.

❀

Virtues and Happiness Research

If the idea that practicing virtues can make us happy sounds more spiritual than scientific, you may be surprised to learn that the Positive Psychology Movement has some hard research to back up this claim.

The best-known research is described in the book *Authentic Happiness*, by Martin Seligman of the University of Pennsylvania. In his groundbreaking study, Seligman asked volunteers to do one of five different tasks. At the beginning of the study, and for six months after, they also took an online happiness/depression assessment to measure their state of mind.

Of the five tasks, one was supposed to be an "inert" or "placebo" activity. As expected, it had a small and short-lived effect on the participant's happiness. One of the other initial activities also had a small effect that lasted slightly longer.

Three activities, however, had a significant effect on the participant's happiness that lasted longer than expected.

In the one that had the strongest immediate effect, participants were given a week to write and then deliver a letter of gratitude – in person – to someone who had been especially kind to them but had never been properly thanked. These people's happiness went up dramatically right after the exercise, and then slowly returned to normal over a six month period.

Gratitude, of course, is a core virtue, so it should not surprise anyone that such an intense expression of it would have a positive effect on a person's feelings, but that this positive effect could last up to six months gives us reason for encouragement in our own lives.

The two other exercises had results that actually *increased* over time.

In the first, participants were asked to take an inventory of 24 "character strengths" that allowed them to identify five top "signature strengths." They were then asked to use one of these strengths in a new and different way every day for one week.

As I mentioned a moment ago, when psychologist use the term "signature character strengths" what they are *really* talking about are *virtues*. "Character strengths" sounds so much more scientific and less spiritual than the word "virtues", but look at their list:

Wisdom and knowledge: Creativity, Judgment, Curiosity, Love of Learning, Perspective
Courage: Bravery, Perseverance, Integrity, Enthusiasm
Love: Intimacy, Kindness, Sociability
Justice: Sense of responsibility, Fairness, Leadership
Temperance: Forgiveness, Humility, Caution, Self-control
Transcendence: Appreciation, Gratitude, Optimism, Humor, Spirituality

All of these "strengths" fit our earlier description of virtues. So in this exercise, participants were being told, "look, you have these five virtues that you are really good at. Now go out and be creative in finding new ways to practice them every day for a week."

The thing about practicing virtues is that, not only does it feel good, but it strengthens the virtues, making it even easier to practice them in the future. No wonder these people's happiness increased over time instead of drifting back down to its original level.

They were stepping beyond the bounds of happiness (the experience of virtue) into the realm of *joy* (the experience of *increasing* one's virtues).

So here is a case where science has measured a significant increase in a large number of people's happiness as a result of practicing a virtue. Who says science and religion can't agree?

The final exercise is a little more subtle in its mechanism. Participants were asked to write down three things that went well each day—and their causes—every night for a week.

We don't necessarily think of self-knowledge as a virtue, but of course it is. In order to fulfill the requirements for this exercise, the participants would have to go through a mini-version of the Internal Consultation exercise I described earlier in this book. They would have to ask themselves what made them feel good that day, which means they would have to explore their feelings and their causes. They would then also have to consider the degree to which they were or were not responsible for those feelings. This is a level of introspection that many people never take the time to experience. It sounds so simple, but after doing it for a week many of the participants would be more self-aware than ever before. No wonder they had the greatest long-term gains in overall happiness.

So what the science of Positive Psychology *can* do is give us graphs and numbers to prove that practicing virtues can make us happier and more content. What Positive Psychology *can't* do, however, is explain that the *reason* why practicing virtues makes us happy is because it satisfies our longing for God; it is the path to becoming our true selves.

Right now, "Transcendence" which is the longing for the Divine, is just one more "strength" at the bottom of their list of twenty-four character strengths. That's OK. Someday science will move the Transcendent from the bottom of the list to the top, and realize that our longing for God – *not* the search for pleasure – is the focal point of our lives.

In the mean time, we can take what science has to offer as proof that we are on the right track, and make a conscious choice as to which virtues *we* want to practice.

88

Where to Start

So which positive sensations do you want to start feeling first? What virtues do you want to invite into your life?

I know, I know. We all want to invite love into our lives, but that is the wrong place to start.

Yes, love is a good thing, but if you put your energies into attracting love into your life—when that has already been your focus since the day you were born—then you are likely to just continue the same old patterns and get yourself into trouble.

Remember, true love is an attraction to a person's constellation of virtues. It is a *meta-virtue* if you will – the virtue of being attracted to virtues. What you want to do is develop your love for *specific* virtues within yourself. It is the virtue of love, but targeted at other virtues, not people.

If you say, "I want to become a more loving person," for example, what you are saying is that you want to recognize, identify and be attracted to every virtue that you see expressed in the world of creation.

In practice, however, you would likely use this goal as an excuse to become emotionally enmeshed with anyone and everyone who expressed even a glimmer of a virtue.

Becoming loving is the goal of a lifetime, not the first step in the process. There are *other* virtues that I recommend that you focus on first. These are core virtues that create the spiritual environment that will make it easier to practice any virtue, including love. I believe they are essential for spiritual healing and growth.

These are honesty, forgiveness, compassion and faith. Honesty and openness help us uncover the painful emotions that we are carrying inside.

Forgiveness allows us to free up the resentments that are keeping our negative emotions locked in place.

Compassion helps us feel connected with all of our fellow children of God, and faith heals our relationship with a God who truly is on our side.

These four virtues may not resonate with you at first glance, but give them a chance. In Book 2 of this series, I am going to describe them to you in a way that I hope will inspire you to appreciate them and, eventually, even *long* for them.

⊗

Whether you choose these four virtues and move on to book two, or you pick your own favorite virtues to explore, practice and enjoy, I want to toss out one simple idea that will make it all much easier: celebrate the process.

No physical pleasure can compare with the joy of spiritual growth. But if we never acknowledge the progress we are making, we can't celebrate it. If we let perfectionism establish goals that are impossible to achieve, then we never let ourselves say "I did it!"

Before you begin the process of replacing shame with joy, and unhealthy behavior with spiritual activities, think a little about how you might celebrate the baby steps you will take on the way there.

Here are some ideas:
Set short-term goals that can be easily met
    (because success leads to more success).
Find someone you can celebrate with.
Give yourself appropriate rewards for success.
Keep a journal of the things you did right.
Say prayers of gratitude for every temptation avoided.

In short, *pay attention,* and know that simply taking that first step on the right path is the hardest part of the journey. Once you do, you can fill your life with the joy of knowing that every day you are moving a little bit closer to God.

❀
Summary and Conclusion

For such a short book, we've covered a lot of ground, so here is a brief summary of the main points I've made:

God is love, and our longing for God is expressed through our search for love. Our emotional sensations tell us about the presence or absence of virtues such as love, but only if we know how to interpret them.

Our life history has caused us to misidentify love, and many of God's other virtues. Instead, we have mistaken the sensations associated with fear and shame for love. The close association between love, sex and shame has caused us to become trapped in shame spirals in which we try to numb our feelings of shame by engaging in behaviors that temporarily distract us from shame, but ultimately increase it.

We can break shame spirals and heal shame by using joy rather than shame to motivate our change in behavior, by facing and overcoming our unrealistic and crippling perfectionism, by being present and listening to the messages that our emotions are trying to send, and by focusing on developing our virtues instead of trying to find love by repeating our old patterns.

Our emotions tell us about the virtues we experience, and painful emotions tell us about the virtues that are missing from our lives.

By developing our virtues, we can fill the spiritual holes in our lives and gain access to a whole range of spiritual sensations that are more rewarding than the physical sensations we pursued before.

If these ideas have made sense to you, and you are ready to start focusing on what you can do to make your life better instead of how to stop doing the things that have gotten you into trouble in the past, then I encourage you to check out the other books in this series, described on the following pages.

An Introduction to Book 2:

❈

Four Tools of Emotional Healing

In *The Secret of Emotions*, we learned that we are all look-ing for Love, Security and Excitement, but our early experi-ences with these virtues left us ill-equipped to actually recog-nize them when we found them. Instead, we have developed patterns that led us to Shame, Secrecy and Fear.

We also realized that it is much more difficult to *unlearn* negative old patterns than to *learn* positive new ones. That is why, in book 2, we will shift our focus to trying to learn four positive core virtues that are essential for spiritual and emo-tional healing: Honesty, Forgiveness, Compassion and Faith.

Here are some excerpts from the introduction of each virtue to give you a taste of what we will be learning:

Honesty gives us the capacity to see what was missing.
Forgiveness gives us permission to speak it.
Compassion gives us the ability to understand it, and
Faith gives us the opportunity to turn it over to God.

Virtues have often been spoken of as though they were burdens. They were seen as effort you put forth on behalf of someone else — to make *their* lives better, not yours. To be honest, for example, was to lose the advantage of deceit. To forgive was to let go of revenge. Compassion meant taking care of others at your own expense, and faith was something you had to feign in order to please an angry God.

No more.

My hope is that by the time you finish reading this section, you will be so enamored of the beauty and power of these virtues that you will hunger for them, and long for the day when you can experience even a glimmer of any one of them in your daily life. These four virtues save lives and restore souls. You need them, and if you read, think, meditate and pray about them, you will discover that you really, really *want* them too.

❀

Honesty

The kind of honesty I'm referring to is not about not stealing (though that is important) nor is it the tactless honesty that encourages you to say hurtful things to others. It is, instead, a tool for self-discovery. It is the kind of honesty that allows you to see yourself accurately, acknowledge the things that have happened to you, and take responsibility for your own future.

I use the word honesty to represent a constellation of virtues that includes openness, truthfulness, an ability to discern what is real and speak about it without shame, and with the courage to risk being oneself....

❀

Forgiveness

There is a way station on the road between uncovering a source of pain and healing it that many people try to ignore. That way station is called anger. You can pass by it in a moment, or set up camp and spend your whole life there, but either way, you can't get from pain to serenity without going through it.

How long you stay there depends, not on how deep your pain is, but how well you understand the nature and power of forgiveness....

❀

Compassion

If you want others to be happy, practice compassion. If you want to be happy, practice compassion.   — *The Dalai Lama*

When we think of practicing compassion, we tend to think of it as an obligation. We are compassionate for the sake of someone else. As the quotation above suggests, that is only half the equation. The practice of compassion offers us three gifts that are central to our spiritual and emotional healing: a sense of connection, a feeling of transcendence, and a source of wisdom....

❀

Faith

Faith helps us replace our need for *excitement*, which is often generated by fear and uncertainty, with *enthusiasm*, which is generated by faith, hope and trust.

There are three aspects of faith that I want to address, and none of them involve a specific religion or doctrine. They aren't about holding on to a belief, or pledging love to one Messenger of God versus another. They are about reflecting an attitude.

These aspects of faith invite us to: maintain an attitude of openness to the unknown; anticipate the good; and trust that everything will work to the good in the long run....

An Introduction to Book 3:

🕸

Longing for Love

In book 3, we take what we have learned about the nature of our emotions and apply it to the practical goal of recognizing, building and keeping healthy relationships. The first half of the booklet focuses on preparing ourselves to recognize true love, as opposed to the many substitute emotions that draw us into relationships, including fear, shame, need, pity, attachment and loneliness. The second half addresses the many temptations that can sabotage a relationship once it has begun.

Here are some of the headings in this book, followed by a few excerpts on assorted topics just to give you an idea of what will be addressed and how:

Part 1 How Do I Find the Right Person?
    Intimate Friendships
    How to Recognize Virtues in Others
    Loneliness and Anxiety
    Other Basic Advice for the Search
    Choosing Intimacy over Intensity
    Other Sensations We Mistake for Love
    Building a Healthy Relationship
Part 2 Dealing with Temptation
    Resisting Unhealthy Behaviors
    Practical Advice for Dealing with Attractions
    Dealing with Inappropriate Desires
    The Power of Denial

How Do I Find the Right Person?

The problem with most relationship-advice systems is that they assume that we are rational people and then give us rational advice as to how to attract another rational person.

But we aren't rational. If we were, life would be much easier, but our behavior doesn't often proceed from our logical minds – no matter how much we may want to believe that it does.

What we generally do as we move into adolescence is look around and see who we are attracted to – and by *attracted* to, I mean who it is that makes our hearts go pitter-patter. We observe the patterns created by these attractions and, either consciously or unconsciously, develop an image of our perfect mate.

We then go out looking for someone who matches that image. Once we find them, we rationalize our attraction with whatever explanation makes sense to our values.

From that point on, we can read any advice book, painstakingly fill out any worksheet, and check off any checklist, and still only see what we want to see....

✧

A Word about Loneliness

One of the many nice things about developing intimate friendships is that when we have friends, we are less likely to enter into unhealthy romantic relationships simply to avoid feeling lonely. Of all of the sensations that are mistaken for love, perhaps "not lonely" is the most common, and the most empty.

In order to understand loneliness, we need to understand why it is we feel the need to be around people in the first place. For me, there are two reasons. The first is that I need other people to mirror back to me who I am. It is like the puzzle: if a tree falls in the forest and no one hears it, does it make a sound?

If I am creative, or of service to the world and I have no one to share it with, how do I know if I am really creative or not? How do I know I've been of service? God does not generally whisper in my ear or pat me on the back, so I have come to rely on other people to tell me when I am doing well. In a sense, I make other people the mediators of God's approval. I subconsciously try to please God by impressing the people around me.

The second reason I need to be with people is closely related to the first. I have a deep longing to exercise my spiritual capacity; to practice the virtues that God gave me. But most human virtues have to do with how we interact with other souls. I cannot be kind in isolation. It is difficult to be of service while hiding in my room. Generosity, forgiveness, compassion, patience, respect, cooperation, these all involve other people.

So we need human contact, not just to receive positive feedback, but to develop our spiritual potential through the process of giving of ourselves....

❈

A Word about Anxiety

Loneliness and anxiety often appear together and both can cause a level of desperation in our search for healthy relationships, so let me explain the connection and offer some remedies.

When I describe shame, I compare it to the sensation of unexpectedly stepping off of a curb. It is the uncomfortable feeling that you are suddenly falling away from God, virtue, and your highest potential. We feel it when we have just done, or are contemplating doing something that is not in harmony with our longing for God. If we think about it for a moment, we can name exactly what behavior we are ashamed of.

Anxiety, on the other hand, is the result of a long, slow drift away from God and our spiritual potential. There is no single action or activity that has severed our feeling of connection with God. Rather, we simply wake up in the morning and sense that something is not quite right, that we are heading in the wrong direction; that something bad is going on, but we can't quite put our finger on it.

Psychologists accurately characterize anxiety as a low-grade fear response. What they haven't quite grasped is *what* it is that we are afraid of. Many people feel anxious when there is no rational reason to be afraid. Their material needs are met, their jobs are lucrative, their family is fine, their health is good, and yet they are still anxious.

This is because the fear at the root of anxiety is not about our physical well-being, but our spiritual progress. Anxiety is the subconscious awareness that our longing for God is not being attended to. If we neglect our relationship with God, then we run the risk of drifting farther and farther away from our spiritual reality. We lose contact with the Foundation of our identity and the Source of our virtues. There is nothing in life more terrifying than this....

❀

Other Sensations We Mistake for Love

When we choose intimacy over intensity, we are choosing to base our relationships on true love rather than fleeting sensations.

True love, as I defined it earlier, is the recognition of, admiration for and attraction to the attributes of God in another person. There are, however, many emotional sensations that can masquerade as love. I have already talked about fear and shame. Others include need, pity, lust, and attachment, along with many subtle variations of love itself.

An exploration of the many emotions that we mistake for love will increase our awareness of the subtle differences between them. This exercise in emotional semantics will help us recognize the subtle differences between *other* similar emotions. The better we become at discerning the difference between emotions, the richer our emotional and spiritual lives become....

The Power of Denial

Denial is the ability to block from our conscious awareness anything that we do not want to be able to see.

Humans are amazingly good at this.

If you have gotten this far in this book and are thinking to yourself "I'm so glad that I don't have any unfinished business or unhealthy attractions to deal with," or if you don't think you have any problems, and that all of your choices are completely rational, then there is a 99.9% chance that you are suffering from denial....

88

Find a Therapist

I'm sorry. No matter how helpful I try to make these books, they will not be a substitute for a good therapist. I know that this will be disappointing to many of you, and absolutely terrifying for others. But if your life is not going as well as you would like, then finding an objective, compassionate person to consult with about it will do you a lot of good. It doesn't replace prayer and meditation, but then prayer and meditation don't replace consultation either.

Having a real live person look into your eyes and say, "You have a right to feel that way" can break through more layers of denial and fear than a hundred books, so give it a try....

❈

About the Author

Justice Saint Rain is the author of several books that blend psychology with spiritual insights. He is both a writer and an artist, and has been producing a line of spiritually-oriented material for over 30 years. He currently lives with his family on a farm in Southern Indiana.

He does not do life-coaching or consultations by phone or e-mail, but he does have a FaceBook page called *Love, Lust and the Longing for God*, and will be happy to try to answer questions and respond to comments posted there.

Forthcoming books in this series:

Book 2: Four Tools of Emotional Healing

There are four virtues that form the core of emotional healing and nurture our spiritual life.

From the Introduction:

Honesty gives us the capacity to see what was missing.
Forgiveness gives us permission to speak it.
Compassion gives us the ability to understand it, and
Faith gives us the opportunity to turn it over to God.

Book 3: Longing for Love
An Unconventional Relationship Guide
How to Recognize and Nurture Healthy Relationships
When Your Heart Keeps Leading You Astray

From the Introduction:

The problem with most relationship-advice systems is that they assume that we are rational people and then give us rational advice as to how to attract another rational person. But we aren't rational. If we *were*, life would be much easier.

Love, Lust and the Longing for God
A Spiritual Guide to Emotional Healing
A groundbreaking exploration of the spiritual roots of our emotional drives. This single volume includes all three books of the *Longing for God* trilogy (*Secret of Emotions* plus the two above), along with over 30 pages of additional resources.

Available from:
SecretofEmotions.com and Amazon.com

Join the conversation at:
www.justicesaintrain.com